SATURDAY EVERYDAY

9 Simple Steps to Live your Best Financial Life

Michael Crews, MBA, CFP®

Copyright © 2019 Michael Crews, MBA, CFP®.

All rights reserved. No part of this book may be used or reproduced by any means, graphic, electronic, or mechanical, including photocopying, recording, taping or by any information storage retrieval system without the written permission of the author except in the case of brief quotations embodied in critical articles and reviews.

This book is a work of non-fiction. Unless otherwise noted, the author and the publisher make no explicit guarantees as to the accuracy of the information contained in this book and in some cases, names of people and places have been altered to protect their privacy.

Archway Publishing books may be ordered through booksellers or by contacting:

Archway Publishing
1663 Liberty Drive
Bloomington, IN 47403
www.archwaypublishing.com
1 (888) 242-5904

Because of the dynamic nature of the Internet, any web addresses or links contained in this book may have changed since publication and may no longer be valid. The views expressed in this work are solely those of the author and do not necessarily reflect the views of the publisher, and the publisher hereby disclaims any responsibility for them.

Any people depicted in stock imagery provided by Getty Images are models, and such images are being used for illustrative purposes only. Certain stock imagery © Getty Images.

ISBN: 978-1-4808-7976-8 (sc)
ISBN: 978-1-4808-7975-1 (hc)
ISBN: 978-1-4808-7977-5 (e)

Library of Congress Control Number: 2019910162

Print information available on the last page.

Archway Publishing rev. date: 02/17/2020

To my sweet wife, Melissa, and to my children, Clayton, Kylie, and Caroline, who make my life the best.

The material in this book is educational and general in nature, does not take into consideration the reader's personal circumstances, and is therefore not intended to be a substitute for specific, individualized financial, legal, and tax advice. The opinions expressed in this material do not necessarily reflect the views of LPL Financial. Tax laws and provisions are subject to change. For advice specific to your own personal circumstances, we suggest that you consult with qualified financial, legal, and tax professionals. The author, Michael Crews, MBA, CFP® and LPL Financial do not offer tax or legal advice or services.

All entities, websites, and programs mentioned in this book are not affiliated with nor endorsed by the author, Michael Crews, MBA, CFP® or LPL Financial.

Any experiences described within are for illustration only, and may not be representative of any future experience of our clients, nor considered a recommendation of the advisor's services or abilities or indicate a favorable client experience.

Hypothetical examples are for illustrative purposes only, and are not representative of any specific situation. Your results will vary. Any hypothetical rates of return illustrated do not reflect the deduction of fees and charges inherent to investing. Individual results will vary.

There is no assurance that the techniques and strategies mentioned are suitable for all individuals or will yield positive outcomes.

All investing involves risk including loss of principal.

Investing in mutual funds involves risk, including possible loss of principal. Value will fluctuate with market conditions and may not achieve its investment objective. Index funds are subject to index tracking error.

Variable Annuities are suitable for long-term investing, such as retirement investing. Withdrawals prior to age 59 ½ may be subject to tax penalties and surrender charges may apply. Variable annuities are subject to market risk and may lose value.

Contributions to a traditional IRA may be tax deductible in the contribution year, with current income tax due at withdrawal. Withdrawals prior to age 59 ½ may result in a 10% IRS penalty tax in addition to current income tax.

The Roth IRA offers tax deferral on any earnings in the account. Withdrawals from the account may be tax free, as long as they are considered qualified. Limitations and restrictions may apply. Withdrawals prior to age 59 ½ or prior to the account being opened for 5 years, whichever is later, may result in a 10% IRS penalty tax. Future tax laws can change at any time and may impact the benefits of Roth IRAs. Their tax treatment may change.

At the time of printing, Michael Crews was a registered representative with, and securities and advisory services are offered through LPL Financial, a registered investment advisor, Member FINRA/SIPC.

Contents

Acknowledgments xiii
Introduction xv
Principle 1 More Money Coming In Than Going Out 1
    Cash Flow 1
    Budgeting Techniques 6
    How the Budget Will Change in Retirement 11
    Emergency Fund 13
Principle 2 Pay Yourself First 17
    Investing the Excess, Identifying How Much and Where
        to Save 18
    Types of Money 18
    To Roth or Not to Roth 21
    Investments 23
    Passive Investments 24
    Active Investments 26
    Fundamental versus Technical Analysis 29
    Valuation of a Stock 31
    Annuities—The Good, the Bad, and the Ugly 33
    Diversification 36
    Golden Eggs—Principal versus Interest 37
    Contributions versus Rate of Return 39
Principle 3 Replace Your Paycheck 41
    When You Turn Off the Paycheck, You Have to Be Able
        to Turn On Other Sources of Income 41
    Understanding Lifetime Income Sources 42

Social Security 43
Social Security Disability 47
Spouse Benefits 48
When to Begin Social Security Benefits 48
Taxes on Social Security...50
The Defined Benefit Pension Plan 51
Defined Contribution Plans 52
Lump Sum versus Annuity Payment Options 53

Principle 4 Fund the Gap 55
401(k) Pretax—Matching and Contributions 56
Inside the 401(k) 56
After-Tax Contributions 57
401(k) Loans..58
Retirement Is All about Cash Flow 58
Living Longer 59
Health Insurance Reduces Cash Flow 60
Medicare 60
Medicare Gap Plans 62
Retiree Medical Insurance 64
Consolidated Omnibus Budget Reconciliation Act
    (COBRA)..64

Principle 5 Climbing Mount Everest 67
The Same Accumulation
    Strategies Won't Work in Retirement 68
Distribution Planning Impact..70
Cash Flow Is More Important Than Interest Rate Savings 72
Time-Based Segmentation 73
Systematic Withdrawals 74
Importance of Separating Income and Growth Assets.........74
Should I Use Pretax or After-Tax Money for My Income
    Plan? 75
Sustainable Withdrawal Rates..76
Monte Carlo Simulation 76

Sources of Lifetime Income 77
Principle 6   One Shot to Get It Right 79
　Income Strategies 79
　Essential versus Discretionary Income 79
　The Solution: The Quadrant Strategy 80
　Quadrant 1—The Emergency Fund 81
　Quadrant 2—Lifetime Income Sources 81
　Quadrant 3—The Growth and Inflation Assets 82
　Quadrant 4—Estate Planning 83
　Quadrant Strategy 83
　Why Invest in Two Strategies 84
　Why After-Tax Assets Should Be Positioned for Growth
　　Rather Than Income 85
　How to Draw Up Your Own Plan 85
Principle 7   A Bucket of Taxes 87
　The Tax Bucket 87
　Age Rules 90
　Retiring Too Early 90
　Retiring Too Late 91
　Age 59½—Diversifying the 401(k) 92
Principle 8   Maximizing Leftovers 95
　Estate Planning 96
　Last Will and Testament 96
　Durable Powers of Attorney 97
　Medical Powers of Attorney 100
　HIPAA Authorization and Release 101
　Directive to Physicians / Living Will 102
　Declaration of Guardian in the Event of Later Incapacity
　　and Need of Guardian 103
　What to Expect from an Estate-Planning Attorney 104
　Other Ways to Transfer Assets 105
　The Importance of Elder Law Planning 106

Principle 9 Live a Life without Limits 109
   A Great Example: Megan Getrum..110
   What It Means to Live a Life without Limits 111
   How Will You Spend Your Time during Retirement?......112
   Finding New Challenges..113
   Financial Health Includes Your Health................................115
   What Will You Be Remembered Most For?........................116
Conclusion..117
Works Cited..119

Acknowledgments

Special thanks to the following:

My wife, Melissa, for encouraging me to complete the process and giving me the time to do so.

My business partner, Chris Scarborough, CFP® for his contributions to the retirement strategies developed for our clients, which greatly contributed to the content of this book.

My mentor, Sue Ricker, for exposing me to the industry, transferring her knowledge, and giving me a once-in-a-lifetime opportunity to help others.

My coworkers for always listening and motivating me to finish the book!

My parents, Wes and Cassie, for being great examples.

My brother Wesley for coming over each week to collaborate on ideas and life.

My sister Jennifer for allowing me to share her story.

My mom, Cassie, for being the first to read my manuscript and give me honest feedback.

My author coach, Ann McIndoo, who helped me get this book out of my head and on paper.

Special thanks to Larry Hornbeck, PhD, Johnny Garrett, Rick Pooler, Ernest Marcos, Erin Peirce, Mark O'Briant, Craig and Debbie Fisher, Jo Umberger, and Leonard and Diane Getrum for their interviews and contributions to this book.

And most of all, thank you to all my incredible clients who have trusted me with their financial futures.

Introduction

> The secret of getting ahead is getting started.
>
> —Mark Twain

What do you imagine when you think of Saturday mornings? For me, Saturdays are a chance to wake up extra early and enjoy the freedom to do whatever I want. I think of taking a drive with the windows down and listening to music with a feeling of freedom.

Saturdays are an escape from school, work, and "have to" tasks. I enjoy the excitement of wanting to capture the day and not let it slip away. I look forward to packing in the activities to live life to the fullest. To me, Saturdays are invaluable.

I think having more Saturdays sounds great, and having every day be Saturday sounds even better. *Saturday Everyday* is an easy read and overview to motivate you to get started on your way to making every day be your own self-designed Saturday. Just knowing you are taking the right steps to take charge of your own finances will energize and excite you about your life. You will awaken each day more confident and ready to pursue your passions, instead of just working for a paycheck.

There are many books about building your own real estate empire or becoming your own boss and escaping the nine-to-five grind. This is not that book but rather a collection of simple yet powerful principles that if followed may help you create financial freedom and more Saturdays. These principles will prevail, even if you decide to become a real estate tycoon, win the lottery, or evolve into the next Steve Jobs. The very nature of principles means they are applicable in a broad set of circumstances and are timeless. These principles will still be relevant to your grandchildren who want to create financial freedom.

First, let's gain a clear picture of what you'd really want if you had financial freedom. How do you define your Saturday? What does Saturday mean to you? What types of activities do you look forward to doing? The very idea of retirement is changing rapidly from the traditional retirement that your grandparents experienced. Take a moment and think about how you would spend your time if you no longer needed to work for a paycheck. What would you do that you can't do while you're working?

In retirement, you can do things for more fulfilling reasons, rather than for a paycheck. So what fulfills you? Do you like helping others, donating your time to charity, spending time with family, working on restoring cars, wood carving, or traveling?

To get to the core of these questions, sometimes it means you have to answer questions about your life's purpose. How will you be remembered? If you could fast-forward and hear what others say about you at your own funeral, what do you hope they will say? The answers to these questions may take some soul-searching, but they will help you identify your core values and your life's purpose. Once you have identified those things in life that really fulfill you, you will require more free time to reap the rewards of such efforts.

This book can give you the greatest gift—the gift of financial freedom. It will teach you the key lessons that will enable you to plan and be prepared so you can create thousands more Saturdays, doing exactly what you love to do every day. Make sure you take some time to write a list of what you're passionate about, and post it somewhere that you'll see it every morning.

Now is the time to get your retirement on track. Serving as a CERTIFIED FINANCIAL PLANNER™ professional over the last fifteen years, I have conducted more than ten thousand face-to-face financial-planning meetings with clients and have managed more than half a billion dollars in client assets as of August 2019. During this time, I've been able to identify key principles that can help you manage your money and make better decisions for your future.

For me, financial planning is a passion. When I'm able to truly help others at some of the most crucial times in their lives, it feels like one of my Saturdays! Therefore, I've identified nine building blocks, or principles, that will have the most impact on your success and experience in retirement.

Random life events do happen and can create a significant financial impact. Plan for what you know will happen, such as bills to pay and groceries and monthly expenses. Plan for what you would like to happen, such as a vacation. Then plan for the unknown. These unplanned life events include, but are not limited to, the following:

- job layoffs
- health changes
- job transitions
- disability
- death of a family member or breadwinner
- caring for an elderly parent or a disabled child
- the decision to retire early

Any of these events will definitely impact your stress level, regardless of your finances. Can you imagine how high that stress level will rise if you are financially unprepared? Will you be able to navigate these challenges with confidence?

Most people want to make sure they can maintain their dignity during such personal financial disruptions, but a family's reputation and dignity can be shattered when the breadwinner becomes ill or passes away without disability insurance or life insurance. Many lives can be drastically altered by such unfortunate events.

I had a personal experience with this in 2012, when my sister's husband was diagnosed with leukemia. After a two-and-a-half-year battle of doing anything and everything to survive, he passed away, leaving his wife and six children behind.

Fortunately, a year before he'd been diagnosed, I was able to talk to him about how he could not afford to have six children without life insurance. His initial reaction to my recommendation to purchase life insurance was "Not yet." He wanted his cholesterol level to go down before buying a policy so that he could get a lower premium. But then again, life insurance is an absolute necessity when you have a family who depends on you. I explained that he should buy a policy and then get a new one when his cholesterol level reduced. I even offered to pay the premium if he didn't want to. Luckily, he agreed, albeit quite reluctantly, to purchase a life insurance policy. The purchase of life insurance ended up making all the difference and provided the needed protection for his family. My sister was able to pay off their debts and the mortgage, settle funeral costs, and help fund the cost of raising her children. The money enabled her to pay for living expenses while taking time to be there emotionally for her children and mourn the loss of her husband. It also relieved extended family members of the responsibility to help pay those costs for her. At the same time, our father retired and was able to help with her small children. This wouldn't have been possible without the life insurance, as he would have had to continue working to help them financially. Instead, he was able to better help them by spending time with the children, which was much more important at that stage in the grieving process.

As you can imagine, proper planning can help you eliminate these stresses and allow you to live your life with dignity during such critical times. You can't skip over life's potholes in the road, but you can plan for and remove the additional financial stress during those events. It's like getting a flat tire. You can't always avoid it, but if you have road hazard insurance, you can at least avoid the cost of needing to buy a new tire.

I have found ways to simplify the planning process and help others understand their financial plan, which in turn has helped them gain confidence and improve their experience in retirement. I hope to share these insights through this book and certainly hope it will do the same for you.

My focus on finances and my passion for helping others started early, even before I was aware of it. As an eight-year-old, I witnessed my father sitting around a tattered round wooden kitchen table, with overdue bills spread out—covering the entire table. Even at that young age, I sensed the stress he felt, which was evident with one look at him.

I'll never forget when he leaned over to me. Out of what I now understand was complete desperation and in the unlikelihood that I would understand the gravity of what he was about to tell me, he said, "Michael, here's my paycheck after one week of working for $330, and here are the bills I need to pay that total $30,000. Which one should I pay?"

I, of course, didn't know the answer.

How did he get into that impossible position? My father was raised in a loving home of seven children. Although his parents were very hard workers, they lived in relative poverty in a small town in Alabama.

My mother didn't have the benefits of a loving home and was raised in an orphanage.

My parents shared an experience during their childhoods that manifested the level of poverty they experienced. Each at one point had a complete stranger buy a pair of new blue jeans for him or her, to replace the worn-out pair they wore.

To change their circumstances, both joined the United States Air Force, where they met and married. After leaving the Air

Force, my parents were in the best financial position of their lives up to that point. My father had a new job, and my mother had completed nursing school and was hired as a registered nurse. My older brother Wesley was diagnosed with an extremely rare hemophilia, called type 3 Von Willebrand's disease. He required several intravenous transfusions each month to stop him from bleeding. Each transfusion cost more than $5,000.

Even though my father had medical insurance through his employer, it only covered 80 percent of the total amount. My parents struggled to pay the remaining 20 percent of the medical bills, which totaled more than both of their salaries combined.

In an attempt to pay it all, they were forced to use credit cards for household necessities and to pay their other bills.

These experiences gave me a unique perspective at a young age, as I saw how hard my parents worked and how unforeseen circumstances could create extreme financial stress. Financial stress is real, and it can damage your health. At one point, my dad was hospitalized with stomach ulcers. Doctors told him that it was caused by stress, most likely from being completely overwhelmed by the financial issues.

From that point forward, I knew what I wanted in life. I made a commitment to work hard, learn as much as possible, and get a good job so that one day I could help my parents and others learn to avoid those tremendous financial stresses, regardless of their circumstances. At the time, I didn't even know that financial planners existed as a profession, but I knew I wanted to become an expert to be able to help people make the best financial decisions possible. I understood the impact that having a sense of financial empowerment could make. I wanted to help others feel in control of their financial future and gain optimism for what they could overcome and accomplish in their lives. In short, I wanted to help people live their best financial lives.

Principle 1

More Money Coming In Than Going Out

> Acquire things the old-fashioned way: save for them and pay cash.
>
> —H. Jackson Brown (1991)

Cash Flow

If you've picked up this book, then you're motivated to start the journey toward a better financial future. But where should you begin?

The most important and first building block to getting your retirement on track is to confirm you have more money coming in than going out (what is commonly referred to as positive cash flow). It doesn't matter if you're the best investor ever, because if you have more money going out than coming in, you'll eventually fail. Warren Buffett, one of the richest people in America and the icon of great investors, is very frugal. He has always had much more money coming in than going out, even when he was working as a paperboy. His success was not only that he was a great investor but also that he understood the power of positive cash flow. He focused on saving early and spending much less than he earned. That difference has given him the ability to continue to invest much more for the future and accumulate massive amounts of wealth. Yes, he made wise investments and built an impeccable reputation, but it all started with positive cash flow!

You may be eager to start investing and growing your money because—let's face it—that's the fun part of personal finance. However, if you have not confirmed you're spending less than you are making and you've saved an adequate emergency fund (more on this later), then you are simply not ready to start investing; you may be doing more harm than good to your long-term financial future. You must build a strong financial foundation, which makes your investing experience less risky. A solid financial foundation will prevent you from having to take out your investments to plug negative cash flow issues, which could harm the long-term returns on your investments.

It won't do you any good to start investing money for retirement and then the moment an unforeseen event occurs, you have to sell your investment at a loss and potentially pay tax and an early distribution penalty of 10 percent to the IRS. You will learn that by approaching your personal finances step by step and utilizing key principles contained in this book, you can be prepared even when facing difficult financial surprises, such as suddenly needing a new set of tires or unexpected medical bills. A proper financial foundation may prevent you from taking these steps backward in your goal of creating a better financial future. It takes discipline and a methodical approach, but mastering cash flow is what will set you apart from your peers and makes positive cash flow such a powerful first step, before you start saving and investing.

If you ask baby boomers, they will most likely express concern and excitement for their children or grandchildren to begin planning for retirement. They want to get their children started early and often ask me where they should start. I always answer,

"With positive cash flow." It's so important that I'm going to repeat it: if you do not have more money coming in than going out, then eventually you'll fail. So if you haven't mastered managing your cash flow, then it is time to stop procrastinating and make it your number-one priority.

This holds true even in business, as a business must have positive cash flow to survive. A business that is not profitable can survive as long as it has cash, but ultimately, it has to be profitable or it'll run out of resources to get more cash and eventually fail.

So how much do you have coming in? Do you know how much you deposit to your bank account on a monthly basis? Surprisingly, most people have a difficult time answering this question, especially since paychecks began being automatically deposited and many don't see their physical paycheck anymore. Sometimes people have a hard time with this question for a different reason. Many of my clients are senior-level engineers at Fortune 500 companies. In fact, many are in the top 1 percent of engineers in the world. Interestingly, even they have a hard time answering questions about how much income they depend on for their lifestyle. Too often, people start with their gross salary and not their net or take-home. They're usually quick to tell me, "I make over $200,000 a year." I help them understand why starting with gross income does not help them accurately assess their lifestyle and spending habits. They're not actually taking home $200,000 a year, as they have many items on their paycheck that are deducted each pay period. It is common that they only deposit 65 percent of their gross income, which in this case is $130,000. To get from gross income to spendable income, they have to reduce the amount by their 401(k) contributions, health insurance, social security tax, Medicare tax, life insurance, federal tax withholding, and sometimes other deductions. So when they look at their net check, the actual amount that gets deposited is much less—usually about 30 to 40 percent less. The net amount is the real amount of income they get to allocate to support their lifestyle.

Do you know how much you deposit each month?

Now that you understand how much is coming in, where is it going? I think everyone has a natural gut reaction to that question, as most people know they splurge from time to time. But it's important to have a thorough understanding and an awareness of your spending habits, or you can't act to improve them.

First, figure out how much is going to pay mandatory fixed expenses. Fixed expenses are exactly what the term sounds like: an expense with a fixed amount each month, such as rent, house payment, investments, savings, or car payment. Fixed expenses are any expenses that you can tell me the exact dollar amount for today, even though the expense won't occur until next month or sometime in the future.

Create your list of fixed expenses, and then total it up to a monthly amount. Be sure to convert all expenses to monthly amounts. If you have an expense that you pay annually, then divide it by twelve to get the monthly amount. If you pay it quarterly, then divide by four and so on. If you pay per paycheck, then multiply it by the number of pay periods in a year and then divide by twelve. This is probably the one that gets most people confused about creating a monthly budget, especially if they're paid every two weeks. Don't panic. Just multiply by twenty-six and then divide by twelve. The key is to obtain a total for your average monthly mandatory expenses. So if your property taxes are $6,000 per year, then you should take $6,000 divided by twelve to get $500 per month.

Now think of the expenses for which you don't know the exact amount until the expense occurs. If it's something like groceries, dining out, clothes, or filling up the fuel tank, you probably won't know the amount until you're actually in the process of buying it. Let's call that variable expenses. Now take some time and total up your typical variable expenses each month. Be sure to include monthly averages for different types of expenses, such as utilities, food, clothing, health care, child care, travel, charitable donations, tithing, birthday and holiday gifts, and hobbies. Download a sample spreadsheet from my website: Saturday-Everyday.com/expenses.

Identifying your fixed and variable expenses is just the start to realizing how much money is coming in and how much is going out. Notice I didn't discuss the items that are already deducted from your paycheck, as you only need to outline the expenses that are paid out of the net amount you deposit. It's okay. This type of method has become a new popular field of study called behavior finance, which examines how people make decisions about money and ways to structure their finances to encourage different (hopefully better) behaviors and decision-making. By focusing on net income, you are simply eliminating the items that you really don't have much control over, while focusing on the portion that you can control.

Many people close to retirement don't have a budget, but they do remember that early in their careers, they lived on very tight budgets. A lot usually changes near retirement as people become empty nesters with kids off at college or on their own. Suddenly, their salaries are at the peak of their careers, allowing them to earn more than they have ever earned in their lifetime. So many choose not to have a budget, as they easily have more money coming in than going out. After all, if you have more money left over each month, then why would you need a budget?

More money left at the end of the month is great, but if you start the retirement-planning process unable to identify how much you're currently spending on a monthly basis, then you'll usually feel lost as to whether you're on track to retire. A crisis of confidence is common at this stage without a budget. Simply put, if you don't have a budget, then you can't quantify your lifestyle, and you won't have enough confidence to retire. It is difficult, if not impossible, to turn off the comfort of a paycheck if you're not sure you will have enough retirement income to support your retirement lifestyle.

It's not unusual for me to work with people for five to seven years before retirement in order to help them reduce their expenses, track their budgets, and become more confident so they can retire. As people approach retirement, a common but unexpected event usually happens. About three months prior to retirement, soon-to-be retirees have a moment of realization (which usually includes some sleepless nights) when they're confronted with the big question: what am I going to do when my paycheck stops? (More on this when we discuss principle 3.)

Fortunately, if you have done all the planning, you will be able to pull out your budget and reassure yourself with the understanding of what you had coming in while you were working, compared to the amount you will have in retirement. You can then feel confident enough to officially retire.

One client I interviewed retired at the peak of the market in 2007 and experienced the recession firsthand. However, he set out to maintain a certain cash flow requirement in retirement so he could meet his retirement goals of traveling often and golfing as much as possible in many locations around the world. If you asked him, he would tell you he was a workaholic, and the best way to eliminate a habit is to replace it with a new habit. In retirement, golf became his new habit, and in his first year he played more than three hundred rounds of golf. To date, even though he retired at one of the most difficult times, he has been on more than thirty-six international golf trips. He was able to meet his golf goals because he identified his cash flow requirements and protected the income he needed. More on this topic in Chapter 4.

Budgeting Techniques

The *b* word—no one likes to talk about budgeting, mostly because it usually ends up with a feeling of defeat for missed objectives or an argument about who overspent. It is typically done all wrong, looking backward at what money was spent where, rather than what budgeting is supposed to be: looking forward and allocating resources for the future.

At the end of the day, identifying where the money is going will help you understand your spending habits so you can start to allocate your spending differently in the future. Learning *how much* you are spending and where you are spending is a crucial step to a better financial future. It really doesn't matter which method you use, as long as you can identify each area of spending to learn how you could behave differently in the future. That's right, spending is a behavior. In fact, spending is a habit, and just like other habits you want to change, it takes awareness and conscious effort to change.

I learned to master budgeting while in college. It was derived from necessity that I learned to live on very little because I was a financially poor college student. I was fortunate to attend college in Hawaii, but the cost of living was very high. I worked for my dad's business in Texas during the summers to save up for the next school year and then had to make sure those funds would last. I used Quicken to track and budget every penny. In 2000, I was newly married, and we lived on $1,100 per month, of which $475 was used to pay for rent in our married-housing apartment. My wife and I had to make the remaining money last all month for food, dining out, entertainment, gasoline, and car insurance. We budgeted twenty dollars per month for entertainment and learned to live without any extras. Through this experience, I learned that you can live on any budget; it is just a matter of what you are willing to give up in order to achieve it.

One major obstacle to sticking to a financial plan or budget is that couples often differ in what they value. This can easily derail even the best-constructed financial plan. This is when the two need to have a healthy conversation about how to compromise and spend only what is agreed on ahead of time.

Let's talk about some of the resources you have available to help you budget more successfully. Of course, today we have more technology-driven solutions in the form of financial software and apps on our smartphones and tablets that we have not had in the past. There are a lot of great cloud-based financial solutions online, such as Mint.com, Quicken, and youneedabudget.com. Using financial software is probably one of the easiest and best ways to go. Many of them download from your bank account, and some banks provide budgeting software built in to the account. For example, Bank of America offers this solution.

There are two different methods to budgeting. You can start with gross income, but then you will have to deduct payroll taxes, withholdings, and 401(k) contributions. As I've already expressed, I don't recommend this approach.

I recommend you create the budget based on deposits. If you are using cloud-based solutions, great news—this is how these programs are already organized. The programs begin with tracking your deposits and then your expenses.

People also still use a checkbook method, which is simply starting with a balance and writing down everything they spend and deducting that from the starting balance. Unless you have a very particular way of tracking that in the checkbook, it doesn't necessarily help you allocate and plan or save for a vacation you've been working on. But if it works for you, then just continue to do that.

The extreme budgeting example is the envelope method. This is for people who have historically had difficulty with budgeting, so they go to the all-cash method. They take their paycheck; say it's $5,000 per month. They take this $5,000 cash and stick it in all different envelopes, allocating toward all their expenses. I think this is a great exercise for everyone to do once as it really allows you to see graphically where your money is going, but doing it every month can be difficult and time-consuming, especially in our modern society with common use of credit cards and ATMs.

Most financial software will actually download transactions from your bank account with the vendor and expenses already automated; in my experience, many people tend to have more success as they begin using more automation. Of course, you can create a custom spreadsheet, and I've found this is very valuable in financial planning. Usually it will be a replacement for the envelope method. It simply is doing exactly what you would do if you were stuffing cash into each envelope, but you do it on a spreadsheet.

Structured budgeting is another method using multiple bank accounts to track spending, the same way you track categories on your spreadsheet. In structured budgeting, you have a checking account where all deposits go, and then you allocate another checking account for fixed expenses and yet another for variable expenses. At the beginning of the month, let's say your total deposits are $6,000, which goes into one checking account. Then you can set up an automatic transfer on the first of each month of $4,000 to pay for fixed expenses and $500 to savings, which leaves the remaining $1,500 to transfer to your spending account. Therefore, you can focus on the spending account, and when the spending account is gone, your budget is gone. At that point, you have not overspent but have spent all your net income for the month. If you end up transferring dollars from savings, you know that any additional transfer of funds is due to overspending, and you have negative cash flow. This should act as a red flag that more needs to be examined in your spending habits.

Of course, one key component of this type of budgeting is to allocate a certain amount each month that is automatically transferred to savings as a part of your fixed expenses. This is the very essence of paying yourself first.

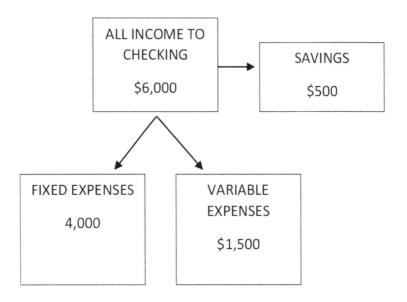

In a client interview, it was recommended that future generations focus on learning how to have a balance in life. He went on to explain, "With my background and my upbringing, I think I was probably more focused on minimizing what I spent my money on, as I didn't make any major purchases or anything like that. It is important to not necessarily fear but develop a respect for what it takes to retire, because it is a big deal. When you think about having enough money to live everyday of your life for thirty to forty years, that's a big deal, and so it would help for you to be educated to know it can be done. There are solid principles that have worked for all kinds of people with lots of different backgrounds that have achieved their goals."

Paying yourself early is a must, and doing it early is just as important. You may have heard of "the rule of seventy-two," which helps calculate how long it will take to double your investments. You simply divide seventy-two by the growth rate or interest rate you plan to earn, and it will tell you how long it will take to double your money. For example, you can usually double your money every ten years if you can earn about 7 percent (72/7 = about 10 years).

The earlier you accumulate, the more this will work for you. For example, if you can save $100,000 by the time you are thirty, then through doubling at a 7 percent growth rate, you will have approximately $200,000 at the age of forty, $400,000 at fifty, $800,000 at sixty, and $1.6 million at seventy. The first $100,000 you save is the most difficult part of accumulating the $1.6 million for retirement. It is also evident that the earlier you can accomplish it, the easier it will be to have more accumulated for retirement. Another way to look at your spending habits is that buying a $50,000 car today costs you $800,000 of future retirement savings.

How the Budget Will Change in Retirement

Listing out your expenses today and getting a really good handle on your lifestyle and what that looks like and what you want that to be will help you shape your budget for retirement. So what are the things that change in retirement? During the initial financial-planning interview, many people tell me they can spend a lot less in retirement, and they plan to spend only half of what they are spending today. As you might guess, in the vast majority of scenarios, this is proven to be an overly optimistic expectation.

Take out a pencil and circle your current expenses that disappear in retirement. You'll find that not much changes. One reduction that people experience is the elimination of your mortgage payment, assuming you purposely plan it that way. For some, they no longer need to buy clothes for work, and the dry-cleaning bill usually shrinks. You may also reduce your commute, since you won't have to drive to work. Perhaps you plan to cook more in retirement and dine-out less, and so the dining bill reduces. Many people are surprised that their expenses don't significantly reduce when they retire.

In fact, many experience an increase in their expenses. Typically, medical insurance costs increase, as does the amount spent on traveling. Retirees often report an increase in the grocery bill, as they have more time to cook. They also may spend more money on hobbies. Since you're no longer busy working, you're hopefully out doing more, and your miscellaneous shopping budget might also increase.

The cost of utilities may go up. The lights, heating, and air conditioning are turned on more because you're at home instead of at work. Therefore, many retirees are surprised that the overall budget gets allocated differently and that they do tend to spend more, not less in retirement.

> Phau states, "Assets should be matched to liabilities with comparable levels of risk. This matching can be done on a balance sheet level, using the present values of asset and liability streams. With asset-liability matching, investors are not trying to maximize their year-to-year returns on a risk-adjusted basis, nor are they trying to beat an investing benchmark. The goal is to have cash flow available, to meet spending needs as required, and investments are chosen in a way that meets those needs. Assets are matched to goals so that the risk and cash flow characteristics are comparable. Modern Retirement Theory argues that funding must be with assets meeting the criteria of being 'secure, stable, and sustainable.'" (W. Pfau 2017)

I recommend you target replacing at least 100 percent of your take-home income in retirement as a starting point.

Emergency Fund

Most agree that everyone should have an emergency fund or rainy-day fund, but it's sometimes more difficult to identify how to build one, how much is enough, and where to invest it. An emergency fund for unforeseen expenses is a critical part of your financial plan, so you don't accumulate credit card debt when the unexpected happens. I'll help you answer each of these questions.

Accumulating an emergency fund is more of an ongoing process than a one-time transaction. It involves a monthly payment to your savings account as if it's one of your regular fixed expenses. Transfer a portion of your income (I often recommend 10 percent) to savings each month. This does not include money that you are saving for a vacation, property taxes, or other major purchase. An emergency fund should be just that, an account for emergencies only, with no prior known purpose.

The typical recommendation is to have about six months of monthly expenses, and a lot of people do not know what that means. They take their annual salary, divide it by two, and think they have identified the amount they need. Let's say you make $100,000 per year, so do you need $50,000 in savings? This is again a place where you want to calculate from net and not gross income. Use the amount you determined you are actually taking home and multiply by six to get the right amount. If the amount of your take-home is $6,000 a month, it is not $50,000 but rather only $36,000 that you need as an emergency fund. So six times your take-home expenses is what you need.

A simple but great question that I hear is "What is an emergency fund? What does that look like?" Sometimes people have their stock account at E*TRADE and think they have an emergency fund. There is a twofold test to confirm you really have an emergency fund: First, the amount has to be liquid, meaning it has to be available for you to get your hands on at any time. It cannot be illiquid, such as real estate interest, land, or something you need to sell in order to be able to access it. Second, it has to be invested in an asset that cannot decrease in value. An investment in cash or cash equivalents is appropriate, such as a bank certificate of deposit (CD) and bank accounts, not a stock or fund that would have price fluctuations. You need access to those funds immediately, at the time you have an unexpected (unbudgeted) medical bill, and that event may coincide with a market downturn. If you had invested your emergency fund in stock, you may find yourself in a bind without enough money to pay the medical bill. Instead, invest your emergency fund where the value cannot decrease.

The issue of making an emergency fund too risky is a more common problem when interest rates are at their lows.

People are having a more difficult time settling for very little interest earned on their emergency fund. Therefore, the tendency to invest it for higher return potential is more prevalent. It's important to change your perspective and view the emergency fund as your solid foundation that lets you invest your other investments more aggressively. You will be able to afford more risk and volatility, as you have a longer time horizon than if you didn't have the emergency fund as a safety net.

For instance, I worked with a client for several years to pay down his credit card balances and simultaneously accumulate a $20,000 emergency fund. Of course, when we set out to accomplish it, we didn't know that this client was going to have major foundation problems with his house. At the same time, he had other emergencies that came up. Fortunately, he had worked very hard to build an emergency fund that he used, instead of accumulating more credit card debt. For him, it was a sense of empowerment instead of unnecessary stress. The experience really built his confidence, and he was able to work hard to rebuild that emergency fund, in case he had another unexpected life event.

Managing your cash flow, making sure you have more money

coming in than going out, allocating your paycheck, and creating a budget and an emergency fund make up the financial foundation to getting your retirement and financial future on track. It may seem basic, maybe even common sense, but you'll learn to appreciate how important it really is as you gain more knowledge about investing and distribution planning in future chapters.

Principle 2

Pay Yourself First

> Twenty years from now you will be more disappointed by the things that you didn't do than by the ones you did do.
>
> —Mark Twain

It's human nature to spend the resources you have and, for many, a little more. However, this habit doesn't mean you'll be financially independent or better off than the average person. Be a leader! Don't be average. Become the person who has his or her finances all figured out. In order to become that person, it's important to create a new habit: paying yourself first. How do you do that? By stashing money in a savings account as an emergency fund each month. Even if you spend your entire paycheck, by having paid yourself first, you will have some money left over for unforeseen expenses in your rainy-day fund.

One thing my dad always talked about when I was young was that he wished someone would have taught him this concept at an early age. Of course, at an early age we don't always heed this type of advice. We often think we will save later when it's easier but then later realize that it never gets easier to save; it only gets harder.

During interviews for this book, I was able to detect common traits of the clients who have been very successful in retirement. Many of these clients were raised in what they refer to as very poor homes, worked hard when they were very young, and often had chores or unpaid jobs to keep the household running. They developed a strong work ethic early and learned the benefits of getting up early and getting things done before school. They all spoke of the importance of saving just a little from the money they earned, regardless of how little the amount. Another common trait was that they started saving at a very early age.

Investing the Excess, Identifying How Much and Where to Save

What should you do next after your emergency fund is funded with six months of your income needs and your balance is steadily growing? This is the point when you are ready to begin seriously investing long term, but where is the best place to start? To answer this question, you must start with building some basic knowledge about types of money and tax benefits. Expanding your knowledge of certain types of accounts and their tax status will help you complete a deeper dive into investing fundamentals.

Types of Money

Financial planners usually separate money into two types, qualified and nonqualified. Qualified assets can simply be thought of as pretax. I like to think of it this way: The IRS has a "qualifying" say in how you spend those dollars, as there are some tax rules to make sure the IRS gets their portion. These are your tax-advantaged accounts; your company may have set aside money in a pension plan for you to receive at retirement, which has very strict guidelines so that tax is deferred until you receive those funds.

Other types of tax-advantage accounts, such as 401(k), IRA, Roth IRA, 403(b), TSA, 457, or anything that has a number (usually representing the number of the tax code), consider those assets qualified or tax-advantaged.

What if you have an account that is not qualified? Then it's no big surprise that those accounts are called *nonqualified*. So everything else: your bank accounts that you have already paid tax on—savings, real estate, cash, stock, and mutual fund accounts—are considered nonqualified assets. You have to pay tax annually on nonqualified assets when you receive dividends and interest payments. You receive a 1099 on those accounts annually, which outlines any capital gains from positions you purchased or sold throughout the year and adds to your taxable income. It's important to know that nonqualified assets are not creditor protected. If you are sued, these assets are up for grabs.

It's necessary to distinguish between these types of accounts, as understanding the tax consequences of each will lead you to answer the next logical question: *Where should I invest?* Tax-deferred savings is typically the place to start, if it is available through a 401(k) plan or similar type of plan offered through your employer. If your employer offers a savings plan, such as a 401(k), you will want to make sure you are contributing at least the amount that the employer matches so you take advantage of all the "free" return they're willing to offer. If they don't match, you still need to do your part and maybe even more to make up for the difference. In fact, many 401(k) plans have automatic enrollment when you are hired. You will be immediately faced with several questions, such as: Do you want to make pretax contributions or Roth contributions? How much do you want to contribute? How do you want to invest your contributions?

The first question about tax-deferred preference usually

appears the most complex, but it can be simplified by one direct question: Is your current tax bracket higher or lower than your tax bracket will be in retirement?

There are obviously several factors to consider so you can answer this question effectively. If you're single and without children, you are potentially paying more in tax than you would if you were married with several dependents. If you're in the beginning of your career and expect your income to increase substantially, then perhaps Roth contributions would be the most beneficial, since you can pay tax today in your lower bracket and then receive tax-free distributions in your retirement years.

Pretax contributions allow you to not pay tax today by contributing to an investment account that gives your money the opportunity to grow, while deferring taxes until you take the money out. Potentially, in retirement you are in a lower tax bracket when you take the money out. Your tax rate may reduce primarily because your gross income can be less or because you no longer have deductions for payroll taxes and other employer benefits, so it doesn't take the same amount of income to get to the same take-home pay in retirement.

Think of that as pretax dollars or qualified money. IRAs are simply another way that you can do the same thing if you do not have a 401(k) available. There are lower limits to how much you can contribute to an IRA. In 2020, it's $6,000, and if you are over age fifty, you can do a catch-up contribution and contribute an additional $1,000 to that IRA. (Visit Saturday-Everyday.com for the most current contribution limits.)

The first tier and part of the plan should be to identify if you have a tax-advantaged account to begin contributing to, such as a 401(k), 403(b), TSA, or 457; 401(k) accounts allow for much higher contribution amounts. In 2020, you can contribute $19,500 plus an additional $6,500 if you are over the age of fifty, so $26,000 a year allows for much more savings capacity. It's helpful to think about different savings choices as buckets, and just like different-size buckets, they all have different capacities. Thinking this way will help you decide which bucket to fill first and which contribution strategy gives you the most tax benefit.

One common mistake is to only save the portion that your company is willing to match. Don't get me wrong—company matching is important; it is free money. For example, if you put in 6 percent, some companies will match you fifty cents on the dollar. Yes, you want to contribute the 6 percent, but you should contribute the maximum, all the way up to $19,500 or $26,000 if over age fifty, so you may build as much retirement savings early on as possible. That way you'll benefit from the power of compounding returns, tax deferral, and account growth for the future.

For example, if you're in the 22 percent tax bracket now and in retirement you're only going to be in the 12 percent bracket because you have less taxable income, then pretax savings as early as possible will be your best friend. Pretax savings can allow you to maximize the difference between the 22 percent and 12 percent brackets and aims to capture that 10 percent savings on the largest amount of money you are seeking to invest and gain on the 10 percent savings difference between tax brackets now before retirement. So when you withdraw the savings you are being taxed at your lower retirement tax bracket of 12 percent. This benefit is only available with proper tax planning, and that is the reason you should pay attention to the types of tax-advantage plans and where you should contribute. Tax planning is one of your biggest opportunities.

To Roth or Not to Roth

I love the title of this section, which is borrowed from a great presentation that I attended by Michael Kitces (visit: kitces.com). It is a crucial question you face when plan for retirement. To contribute to a Roth IRA, you contribute after-tax dollars. You must pay tax today, and then that money grows tax-deferred and allows for tax-free distributions in retirement. In retirement, you can take those dollars out without any taxes on the earning, as long as a few rules have been followed: you have a minimum five-year holding period from the first contribution date, and you have reached age fifty-nine and a half.

Roth IRAs have engendered much debate, and many interesting financial articles have been written that discuss how great Roth IRAs are. Typically, these articles highlight the benefits of tax-free dollars in retirement versus the alternative of contributing pretax dollars into a 401(k) or a traditional IRA.

It's kind of comical to listen to all the arguments about accumulating more wealth on a pretax basis, while the other side is arguing that more tax-free dollars will yield a better retirement. I find these arguments entertaining, as it only boils down to one variable, which is what your tax bracket is today compared to what your tax bracket will be in retirement. For example, if you were to invest $100,000 in a pretax account that grows tax deferred at 10 percent a year, in ten years it would have accumulated $259,374.25 in pretax dollars.

You would have to pay taxes to get those dollars out, so let's say you pay tax at 24 percent, and then the remaining amount would be what you would have left to spend, which would be $197,124.43. Whereas, if you go back in time and make Roth contributions instead, you would have to pay tax today. *That* money would grow 10 percent for that ten-year time period, and you would not have $259,374.25; you would have something less, 24 percent less. Consequently, if your tax bracket today is 24 percent and in the future it is 24 percent, you will end up with the same dollar amount in hand after taxes—$197,124.43.

You should think of Roth contributions when you expect to have more income during your retirement years or you're in a very low tax bracket today and you expect to be in a high tax bracket in the future. If you're a family of five or ten, you may be better off doing Roth contributions because in retirement, you will be empty nesters and have more taxes to pay and maybe without a mortgage to write off.

Comparing your retirement tax projection to your tax picture today will help you decide whether you should contribute to a Roth or not. Of course, the other factor is that we cannot predict what tax brackets are going to be in the future. I do think it's safe to assume that tax brackets will not go down. If you look at the amount of debt that our country has and the need for taxation, most experts agree it's unlikely that you will see lower tax rates in the future than you have today.

One strategy is to contribute pretax dollars, as well as Roth, and give yourself some flexibility by having two pools of money to pull from. This way you can have some taxable and some that is tax-free in retirement, which gives you more options when planning for retirement.

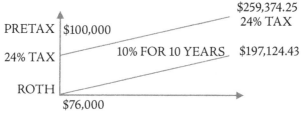

Investments

A common mistake is to spend all your financial-planning time on investments. Be careful not to spend all your time and attention on your investments rather than the overall plan. Doing so is like reading just the owner's manual of your car before taking a trip across the country. The owner's manual is not going to help you with things like where to stop to eat, sleep, get gas, how long it will take to get there, and so forth. Focusing solely on investments is like focusing only on the vehicle without regard to where you are going. Planning your finances is no different. You need a map to know what it will take to reach your destination, and just like the car, it is an important part of the trip (identifying which vehicle meets the terrain/objective), but it is just a part of the requirements and not the entire plan.

Just like a goal that is not written down is only a wish, a financial plan that is not written down is only a hopeful dream. You must write it down to accomplish it. A written financial plan is more than just investment allocation, as it should include your projected retirement income after taxes, which assets will be utilized for income, and which will help you keep pace with inflation. Then you can choose the investments that meet each objective. Typically, investments such as stocks, bonds, and mutual funds, exchange-traded funds, and certificates of deposit are common vehicles chosen for growing your assets. There are two broad schools of thought on how assets should be managed: passive and active.

Passive Investments

Passive investments usually involve a buy-and-hold strategy. Growing in popularity over the last decade are index funds, which are a collection of stocks and bonds that are not actively traded by a manager. Index funds are designed to mimic an index, or baskets of stocks or bonds, in large quantities—typically owning entire sectors of the market or all types of stocks in the US economy. For example, an index fund might make an investment in large, medium, or small companies. A part of the attraction to index funds has been their lower expense ratios, making them cheaper than hiring a manager. Also, based on financial research and historical data, very few active managers consistently outpaced passive investing.

Whether passive or active management is the best approach is still being debated today. Regardless of which camp you want to believe, many times in my seminars I'm asked if buy-and-hold strategies are outdated and if they still work. My standard response is that it depends on what you buy and what you hold. Asset allocation (the different types of investments you own) can determine up to 90 percent of the return you will realize as an investor (Ibbotson 2000).

I found this to be true during the dot-com bubble in 2001 and 2002, when investors who were primarily invested in the dot-com era lost significant portions, and in some cases all, of their funds invested in that sector. Whereas, if an investor were truly diversified, he or she would have owned about fifteen different asset classes in the portfolio.

An asset class is a group of investments that are the same type. Some examples of assets classes are real estate, commodities, large cap, midcap, small cap, international, bonds, international bonds, value, growth, sectors, and emerging markets. Each of these asset classes tends to perform similarly to other holdings in the same asset class. By investing in different asset classes, it provides the investor diversification, as all the investment won't usually move in the same direction, the same amount, and at the same time. This way the investments offset each other, and they may give the investor more consistent, predictable returns than by just investing in one sector. In this manner, you lower your highest possible return, but you also avoid the pitfalls of owning the wrong investment at the wrong time.

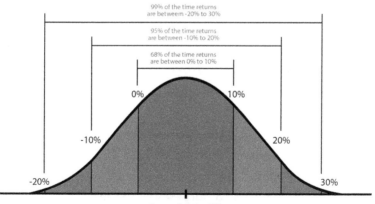

If you expect a 6 percent, 8 percent, or 10 percent return, then what you will notice is that it will require more risk or variability in the portfolio to obtain the higher rates of return. Returns you experience each year that are different from the expected return represent the risk or variance (the returns you get that are not what you expect). This return variance or deviation can be measured and should be a part of your analysis. As an investor, the biggest way you can reduce that risk and have statistics work for you is to become truly diversified, where you do not have too much in one sector or in only one investment and measure the risk of the portfolio for a given expected return.

You'll hear financial planners talk about diversification, because returns can become very predictable, and statistics work in large numbers with different stock sectors.

Active Investments

Active investing means you buy into the idea that you can be in the right investment at the right time. Statistically, it's a very challenging thing to do, and even managers who have consistently been able to do that for years are eventually wrong. For instance, one manager who was able to be in the right place at the right time and beat the market for fifteen years in a row and ranked as manager of the decade then lost much of that return in one single year, 2008. You can read about it here:

https://www.forbes.com/sites/steveschaefer/2011/11/17/end-of-an-era-bill-miller-to-give-up-reins-at-legg-mason-value-trust/#4f45e8ec6032.

Simply being in the wrong place at the wrong time, if you're overly concentrated in a particular position or company and not diversified, can ruin those returns and your retirement. Active managers look for ways to outperform the market or unmanaged benchmarks. There is a statistical measuring stick for you to evaluate active managers, which is called "Alpha." Today, using Google finance online (finance.google.com), there are a lot of tools for you to easily find those statics, so you don't even have to calculate them. Alpha is a comparison of performance of *the managed portfolio*, compared to the unmanaged market, usually the S&P 500 index, so it will be easy for you to compare how much better or worse the active manager performed. The higher the number, the greater the manager outperformed the market. A common question you'll hear if you're looking for active management is: How much alpha is that manager creating?

First, what is Alpha? Alpha is a statistical measurement to compare the return of a portfolio to the benchmark. This makes it quicker for an investor to determine if a portfolio manager was able to beat the benchmark or market index. It is, in general terms, whether the portfolio manager is creating any value or if the investor would have been better just investing in an index or unmanaged basket of stocks. As you begin researching an actively managed fund you will most likely encounter something that resembles the following performance measurements:

	1 year	3 years	5 years	10 years
Alpha*	1.72	1.98	1.20	2.03
Beta*	0.77	0.90	0.92	0.86
Mean annual return	1.23	0.96	1.13	0.76
R-squared*	76.51	87.16	89.16	90.50
Standard deviation	5.44	10.04	9.90	13.85
Sharpe ratio	2.63	1.12	1.35	0.62

*As compared to the S&P500
Hypothetical example for illustrative purposes only. Not an actual investment.

You'll notice that the first line represents the alpha against the standard index for each time period. An alpha of greater than one lets us know that the fund outperformed the benchmark during that time period.

You would also want to look at risk factors standard deviation or variance, which is how far the portfolio returns go outside of what you would expect. Not only would you need to assess how much return you would expect but also how much risk you would be assuming as the investor versus the passive portfolio.

So who is right? Investors have two main investment strategies that can be used to optimize potential returns: active management and passive management. Active management involves researching and selecting individual securities in a fund, with the aim of outperforming the market. The passive approach is to generate a return that is the same as the chosen index, instead of outperforming it (IFSE 2017).

Many believe that while it's possible to beat the market, the chances of doing so are very low. The low odds of success are why Charles Ellis called active management the loser's game and passive investing the winner's game. Maybe this is what prompted Warren Buffett to bet a million dollars that passive investments would outpace active management.

In 2008, Buffett made a million-dollar bet that his simple, low-cost investing strategy would outperform the hedge fund industry. Here's Buffett's original challenge, as detailed by the Long Now Foundation (http://longbets.org/362/): "Over a ten-year period, commencing on January 1, 2008, and ending on December 31, 2017, the Standard & Poor's 500 stock market index (S&P 500) will outperform a portfolio of funds of hedge funds, when performance is measured on a basis net of fees, costs and expenses."

Buffett chose a type of stock mutual fund known as an index fund that tracked the S&P 500 at the time of the contest. Index funds are not actively managed and therefore have lower fees. An index fund is simply a basket of stocks designed to track the returns of the stocks of the five hundred large American companies that comprise the S&P 500. Protégé Partners accepted Buffett's challenge and selected five hedge funds. Hedge funds are managed by Wall Street's best and brightest and therefore are known to have higher fees and costs (Bowsher 2016).

At the end, December 31, 2017, it became evident that Buffett had taken the right side on choosing how to invest.

Mr. Buffett's index fund had earned an annualized return of 7.1 percent for the first nine years. The average of the five hedge funds selected by Protégé Partners had produced an annualized return of 2.2 percent over the same timeframe. The index fund Mr. Buffett chose was up 85.4 percent overall over the first nine years, while the average overall gain of the five hedge funds was only 22 percent (Bollin 2017).

What does this say to us? Buffett's bet highlights a great investing lesson you can benefit from: cost matters in investing. Buffett's bottom line: "When trillions of dollars are managed by Wall Streeters charging high fees, it will usually be the managers who reap outsized profits, not the clients," he writes. "Both large and small investors should stick with low-cost index funds."

Fundamental versus Technical Analysis

Whether looking at financial statements or charts is a better approach for choosing the right investments continues to be a subject of debate. Economists, investors, and money managers tend to differ on whether fundamental or technical analysis leads to better investment results. Any active manager who is trying to be in the right place at the right time uses different methods and tools in order to make predictions, forecasts, and fair-market-value estimates. Traditionally, a fundamentalist or fundamental investor would look at the valuation of a company. However, we are bombarded with arguments for technical analysis with catchy chapter headings such as "Throw Away the Fundamentals and Stick to Your Charts" (Covel 2011). How is the novice investor to know which to believe? We can use Apple as an example (ticker symbol AAPL) to try to help you answer this question.

On August 2, 2018, Apple became the first public company to reach a $1 trillion value or market capitalization. The price reached $207.05 per share, and if you multiply the price by the number of shares outstanding (4,829,926,000), you will calculate a valuation of the company of $1 trillion.

Let's say you had that much cash lying around and you think, "Okay, I'm going to write a check for Apple to own all of Apple's shares for $1 trillion." What would be the question in the back of your mind? Probably, "How much is the company earning?" You can then calculate how long it will take to recoup your trillion-dollar purchase. We look for Apple's net income to see what the payback period would be and how their revenues and their net incomes are growing over time. We would try to predict by asking ourselves, "If I write a check for the company today, how long will it take me to get my money back and what is my return on investment over and above the check that I wrote?"

That is the bottom line to investing in any stock: to value the entire company in realizing that you're just buying a slice of the pie. If you are not theoretically willing to write a check for the entire company and not willing to own the whole thing, then you should not buy any part of it. That is what traditionally comes to mind when we think of fundamental investing and we look through the accounting statements, cash flow, forecasting, and projected cash flows. It is the typical finance approach to investing.

The other approach is technical analysis, which relies on trends, momentum, graphs, and charts. You look at the trends of the stock, look at stock price changes over time, and calculate the average price during a specific period, what is referred to as a moving average. Technical traders take an average daily price for the last two hundred days and use this as a predictor for where the stock price is headed. Some investors can predict trends of where the stock price will be in the future, based on historical trends, but it proves difficult to do consistently over longer periods of time. The model that predicts one market movement may not predict the next, and therefore, a new technical model must be developed. These models usually get created after the fact, which sometimes doesn't do much for growing your account value.

Fundamental and technical analysis are the two primary sets of tools that active managers use. Therefore, if you are investing with a manager, you should understand the philosophy and methods of investing to confirm that it coincides with your comfort level and beliefs about investing.

Valuation of a Stock

How do you know what a stock is worth? Valuing a stock is just like valuing any other asset. If you were to ask a finance person, the standard answer would be, "It is worth its discounted cash flow discounted back to present value." But what does that mean? For example, if you're going to buy a rental home for the very first time, and that home is on the market for $300,000, and you decide to purchase it, is that a good deal or a bad deal? Well, you have to know how much rent you think you can get from it. Let's say you determine that the rent would be $1,800 a month, and you figure out the expenses to be $300 per month, so you will keep the net amount of $1,500 a month. Is $1,500 per month a good investment return on your $300,000 investment? You can simply calculate the return based on your $300,000 and see if it is worth it.

Market Price	Annual Rental Income	Annual Expenses	Net Cash Flow	Return on Cash Flow
$300,000	$21,600	$6,000	$15,600	5.2%
$250,000	$21,600	$6,000	$15,600	6.2%
$200,000	$21,600	$6,000	$15,600	7.8%
$150,000	$21,600	$6,000	$15,600	10.4%

When you look at a company's stock, you should think of it the same way. If you purchase that stock, how do you get money back? It's not in the form of rent but in the form of dividends. Typically, when you value a stock, you are always going to value the dividends, that is, the return of the money to shareholders over time, and then discount it back to today's dollars. What discounting means is that money today is worth more than money in the future.

Would you want me to give you $100 today or $100 ten years from now? I'm sure you are thinking, "I will take the $100 today, thank you." If you must wait ten years for it, you'd probably want $200 for having to wait; otherwise, you'd just take the $100 now. Discounting cash flow means converting future cash flows into today's dollars. For example, if you are going to receive dividends over the next ten years from your current stock portfolio, you will need to discount those future dividends into a present value today to evaluate the current stock price and yield that are in today's dollars.

You do that by taking some form of an interest rate of what you think you can earn on investing, such as 5 percent. So what happens when we discount or move backwards? One hundred dollars ten years from now is only worth $61.39 today. ($100 ÷ 1.05^{10} = $61.39). Restated, it means that you will need $61.39 today to invest at 5 percent annual compounding interest rate to have $100 exactly ten years from now. It is common practice in finance to discount all future investment cash flows into today's dollars so that all alternatives can be more easily compared.

Annuities—The Good, the Bad, and the Ugly

The word *annuity*, based on recent media, has had a negative connotation because there are several annuity investments that can be high in fees, low in benefits, and very profitable for the insurance company. Let's back up a minute and think about what an annuity actually is.

An annuity is a stream of income payments the investor will receive over a certain period of time. Annuities have been around since the beginning of the earliest monetary systems. In fact, people were considered wealthy based on their income per month, rather than their accumulated wealth. People at that time would speak about wealth fully in terms of an annuity or how much income they received per month.

Therefore, think of an annuity as cash flow over a specific period. Which sources of income meet this annuity requirement? There are only three entities that have the size and ability to guarantee payments: government, employers, and insurance companies. One of the major reasons people choose government jobs is for the benefits package offered. Besides great medical benefits, government employment provides lifetime income payments at retirement.

Social Security payments also provide lifetime income payments and are a primary source of retirement income for the majority of the population, even though they weren't designed to do so.

Employers also provide annuities in the form of a pension payment to their employees at retirement. These payments are guaranteed for life by that employer.

If you need to purchase a personal pension plan, the only option is to work with an insurance company that has the financial capacity to provide guarantees of lifetime income. Nobody likes paying for insurance, but sometimes it's necessary to reduce risk. If you can have a guaranteed payment for life, using that form of annuity eliminates the risk of running out of money.

Annuities are complex in the sense that they use mortality tables and interest rates, and it takes some heavy finance equations to even evaluate them. That is what makes it difficult for the average investor to say, "Is this a good deal or a bad deal?" *Comparing* multiple annuities and what is out there in the marketplace, just like you would shop for a CD, you ask, is that a good interest rate? Well, I don't know. What are other banks offering? You have to do the same thing when you evaluate an annuity; see what other insurance companies are offering as a comparison to determine whether or not you are getting a good deal. But an annuity has many more variables to evaluate.

In addition, there are several different types of annuities. An *immediate annuity* gives you payments as the name suggests, immediately. You invest a lump sum and then begin receiving payments immediately.

A *deferred annuity* allows you to invest and have the value grow at some interest rate, to provide you with payments in the future.

There are also *fixed annuities* that work just like CDs at banks, except they are not insured by the bank or FDIC. They are instead backed by the insurance company. They typically offer higher interest rates than CDs to compensate the investor for slightly more risk, as outlined in the fine print, "based on the claims paying ability of the insurance company."

Then, there is an *indexed annuity*, which you can think of as having a floor and a ceiling. It will give you a floor of no risk to principal, no loss, but that also means your earning potential is limited. There is a ceiling, maybe only 4 to 5 percent that you can grow per year, based on some market indexes. That is a way of giving you principal protection with perhaps a little more upside than CD rates today.

There is also a *variable annuity*, which you look to for better control of the investment. If you want to put it in a mutual fund—like investments—but want the company to give you some kind of safety net, a variable annuity will allow you to take some risk in such investments while taking distributions. At some point, if you run out of money, you can still receive lifetime payments as if you hadn't run out.

Those have been popular in past years, not so much recently because interest rates have dropped to all-time lows, which have made it really difficult for insurance companies to make the value proposition attractive.

Then there are hybrids that mix these different features, so you really have to do your due diligence and understand how the annuity works. The top questions to ask are these:

1. What happens if your account reduces to zero?
2. How much income are you going to be left with at that point? (Always ask that question to understand the true benefit of the annuity, which is a lifetime income. Some annuities have income that reduces if the account value disappears.)
3. What happens to my principal?
4. How does the principal grow?

If you answer those questions, you will be able to start comparing the different annuity formats and investment types.

One of the most significant risks to retirees today is running out of money in retirement. Annuities are one solution that has helped retirees avoid running out of money and should be evaluated as a portion of your investment portfolio in retirement. Wade

Pfau points out three reasons why it may make sense to include an annuity:

> Income annuities, as opposed to individual bonds, provide longevity protection by hedging the risks associated with not knowing how long you will live.
>
> Annuities protect from longevity and sequence-of-returns risk and because income continues automatically, they also provide protection for cognitive decline.
>
> Most retirees will not have saved enough to safely immunize their entire lifestyle spending goals, through only bond ladders and income annuities, while still maintaining sufficient remaining wealth to create a liquid contingency fund for unexpected expenses. (2017)

Diversification

How do you allocate and diversify a portfolio? If you are investing in individual stocks and bonds versus using mutual funds, you need to understand your level of diversification, as well as the risk/return exposure. Then, think of how you should go about building it and making sure your portfolio is diversified.

How do you know if your portfolio is diversified? There is a statistical measure called R-Squared. When you go to Yahoo or Google finance, you can look up the investment, and it will say "R to the second power," and it will give you a number. The textbook answer is if that number is 0.8 or higher, then it is considered a diversified portfolio. If it is lower, then it's considered not to be diversified. You may need to use a more powerful tool such as Morningstar to evaluate your individual holdings as a whole portfolio to confirm its r^2 value.

With such tools, you can take a set of different mutual funds and evaluate them holistically to answer these questions: "What is my R-squared number? Is it greater than 0.8 or less than 0.8?" That would be the technical answer to "Do you have a diversified portfolio?"

The other way to evaluate it is to look at correlations of the assets that you own. If you are in the S&P 500 and you say, "I am diversified; I own five hundred of the largest stocks in the US economy," the problem is that most large stocks move together. If the markets are down, your portfolio is down. We can look at several examples throughout our history where that was the case. In 2008, if you were in the S&P 500, even though you owned five hundred stocks, almost all of them were negative.

Having a more diversified portfolio would include asset classes, such as medium-size companies, small companies, small-value stocks, and small-growth stocks, as well as international, emerging markets, bonds, international bonds, real estate, and commodities. You should have as many asset classes in the portfolio as you can so that potentially if some asset classes are down, then others may be up.

Golden Eggs—Principal versus Interest

If you are trying to create retirement income from your investments, one of the questions will be, "Are we spending down our principal?" The traditional investment would be to buy a bank CD that pays 5 percent and factor in and say, "Okay, I have $1 million saved for retirement. If I buy $1 million worth of CDs, then I will have 5 percent or $50,000 a year coming in as interest, and I am not touching my principal."

For example, the story of the golden goose shows that if you take care of that goose, you keep getting the golden eggs, which are the interest. But if we get greedy and want distributions too fast, then we obviously start trying to get the interest faster and kill the golden goose. In other words, you start spending down your principal.

The key principle to understand when you start to spend down your principal is that the necessity to spend more principal each year will only accelerate until you have exhausted the entire portfolio.

For example, if you decide to take out a distribution of $100,000 from your $1 million portfolio that was providing $50,000 prior to distribution, after the distribution it will only provide $45,000 the following year. Now you only have $45,000 coming in per year, and that is not quite enough, so you have to dip in a little more. This process results in a snowball effect, where every year you have to take a little more principal out, and pretty soon you are left with no principal, no interest, and no income.

That is one of the mistakes I have personally seen many retirees make. They overspend early in retirement, start spending down their principal too quickly, and begin the snowball effect. It is like when you are budgeting and you borrow from next month. Now, next month is short, so you have to borrow from the following month, and it just continues on. It is a quick way to run out of money. Think of the golden goose story; protecting your principal and just living off the interest is key.

Contributions versus Rate of Return

If you are saving for retirement, what is the most important variable that will determine how much you will have at retirement—the amount you save annually or the rate of return your investments earn? It seems more conversations are about the rate of return you will earn on your investments, even though the bigger lever to pull for getting more assets at retirement is how much you contribute. This is probably because it requires less personal discipline to earn a little more than to save a little more. Let's face it: it is human nature to conclude that if you can get a higher rate of return, then you can afford to contribute less and enjoy a little more now. This can cause investors to get riskier than they should be in their portfolio, trying to stretch to reach their retirement savings goal. Contributions move the needle the most and will get you to the largest dollar amount at retirement.

Current Value	Growth Rate	Contribution per year	Years	Future Value 30 years in the future
$100,000	5%	$10,000	30.00	$1,096,583
$100,000	6%	$10,000	30.00	$1,364,931
$100,000	**7%**	**$10,000**	**30.00**	**$1,705,833**
$100,000	8%	$10,000	30.00	$2,139,098
$100,000	9%	$10,000	30.00	$2,689,843
$100,000	10%	$10,000	30.00	$3,389,880

Current Value	Growth Rate	Contribution per year	Years	Future Value 30 years in the future
$100,000	7%	$10,000	30.00	$1,705,833
$100,000	7%	$15,000	30.00	$2,178,137
$100,000	7%	$20,000	30.00	$2,650,441
$100,000	7%	$25,000	30.00	$3,122,745
$100,000	7%	$30,000	30.00	$3,595,049
$100,000	7%	$35,000	30.00	$4,067,353

As you can see in the above example, the rate of savings, not the growth rate, is the largest factor in determining the future value of your assets. Growth rates don't move the needle as much as your contribution rate or how much you save each year. Ultimately, there is no shortcut to saving more, rather than chasing higher returns at higher risk levels.

Another example that supports saving early is to examine the outcomes of an investor who begins saving early in his twenties and accumulates $100,000 by the time he is thirty, versus somebody who doesn't start saving until they're forty.

An easy way to think about that difference is to think about the $100,000 saved earning 7 percent, which will double every ten years (Rule of 72). So $100,000 at thirty is $200,000 at forty, $400,000 at fifty, $800,000 at sixty, and $1.6 million at the age of seventy. Just that original $100,000 you saved means you did not have to contribute the other $1.5 million for retirement. Hence, the common-sense advice—the earlier you start and the more you save early on, the more the compounding effect will really set you apart from other people who get a late start. This difference will enable you to have more disposable income later, since you will not have to save the majority of your paycheck trying to play catch up on the early savings years you missed.

Principle 3

Replace Your Paycheck

> My favorite things in life don't cost any money. It's really clear that the most precious resource we all have is time.
>
> —Steve Jobs

When You Turn Off the Paycheck, You Have to Be Able to Turn On Other Sources of Income

The clients I've worked with for five to seven years prior to retirement often do not fully grasp what it means to turn off their paycheck until they're within a few weeks of retirement. I've noticed they begin to listen differently as they start to fully absorb the concept that their paycheck is stopping, and then, as you can imagine, they become acutely interested in what new sources of income they will have in retirement.

During the time period when people are accumulating assets, they always tend to measure their results by their total dollars saved for retirement. They might say they have $500,000 or one million saved for retirement. They measure their progress by the size of their savings but usually have no idea if the amount they have saved is enough.

But when near retirees are actually in the process of retiring, usually within ninety days of their retirement date, they tend to stop talking about how much they have saved and start talking about their wealth in terms of monthly or annual income. The conversation usually goes something like this: "Well, I can get $2,000 a month from Social Security. I can get another $2,000 a month from my pension and $1,500 per month from an annuity I purchased." This is a powerful and important paradigm shift in how they view their accumulated wealth during the retirement process. The realization that their paycheck is stopping causes them to begin trying to add up their monthly income sources to see if they can really afford to retire.

It's a little bit more difficult if you say, "I have $1.5 million saved for retirement. Can I really afford to retire?" You have to put that in concepts of lifestyle, which is usually in the form of monthly income, so you can confirm it will cover your monthly expenses and the additional retirement expenditures such as travel.

Understanding Lifetime Income Sources

Income sources that continue to pay for the rest of your life include pension, Social Security, and investments, depending upon the withdrawal rate you take. Of course, one of the most important questions you will need answered for retirement is "How much can I safely draw from my investments without running out of money?" I'll provide you the framework to answer this question in chapter 7.

It is not an easy question to answer, as you can spend your entire lifetime investigating all the variables that should be evaluated to successfully answer this question. Financial quant Moshe Milevsky, who consults with the Social Security Administration, insurance companies, and pension plan administrators as an actuary, is a great example of someone spending a lifetime answering these types of finance questions. At the age of nine, he lost his father and began playing the fatherly role of taking care of the entire family. His mom asked him the most important question: "How much can the family safely draw from their life insurance money without running out of money?" He has spent the rest of his life dedicated to the subject.

Social Security

For many Americans, Social Security will be a primary source of lifetime retirement income. You can begin benefits as early as age sixty-two, regardless of when you were born, and will receive 70 to 80 percent of your full retirement age (FRA) benefit. Your monthly benefit actually increases five-ninths of 1 percent per month from age sixty-two to your FRA or about 6.6 percent per year. When is your full retirement age for Social Security benefits? It depends upon the year in which you were born. Reference the below chart.

Year of Birth *	Full Retirement Age
1937 or earlier	65
1938	65 and 2 months
1939	65 and 4 months
1940	65 and 6 months
1941	65 and 8 months
1942	65 and 10 months
1943--1954	66
1955	66 and 2 months
1956	66 and 4 months
1957	66 and 6 months
1958	66 and 8 months
1959	66 and 10 months
1960 and later	67

Full retirement age matters because that is the age you can file for benefits and continue to work and receive your full Social

Security payment without a reduction for having earned income. For example, if you were to draw your Social Security check at age sixty-two and continue to work, you would be limited on how much you could earn without reducing the Social Security benefit you were collecting. Your earnings in 2020 are limited to $18,240. For every two dollars you earn over that, they withhold one dollar of your Social Security payment.

If you're self-employed, net income is used to calculate your income, so it's very limiting on what you can earn. But when you're of full retirement age, you can go back to work and earn as much as you want and draw your full Social Security check.

A lot of the rules have recently changed with new legislation. Congress changed the rules on filing a restricted application with Social Security, which allowed individuals to significantly increase the amount of social security benefits they would be able to draw over their lifetime. Congress viewed this strategy as double dipping as it allowed an individual to draw on a spouse's record through *file and suspend* and *restricted application* strategies. The Bipartisan Budget Act of 2015 made these changes and applies to you if you turned sixty-two on or after January 2, 2016. Refer to https://www.ssa.gov/planners/retire/claiming.html for updates.

If you would like to maximize your Social Security benefits, when should you start drawing benefits? If you draw at age sixty-two, it's a lesser amount compared to what you would receive at full retirement age, but you get to start checks earlier.

The important part is that you don't have to wait for your next birthday to start benefits, since your Social Security benefit increases monthly. If you decide not to retire at sixty-two but maybe a few months after, your benefit will be slightly higher by having waited an extra few months. You can also defer Social Security longer than your full retirement age, all the way to age seventy. There are no benefits to starting after age seventy, so absolutely start your Social Security check no later than age seventy.

The reason you might consider waiting to draw your Social Security benefits until age seventy is that the benefit amount starts increasing 8 percent a year from your full retirement age until age seventy. Therefore, your check could be 32 percent higher for the rest of your life by waiting until age seventy. There are three primary reasons why waiting until age seventy make sense.

First, more income. Social Security is indexed to inflation, and you get cost-of-living adjustments. If the check is higher and they give a 3 percent cost-of-living adjustment, then you are getting a bigger increase than if you would have had a lower check amount.

Second, more tax-free income. Fifteen percent of your Social Security check is not currently taxable, as it represents a return of your contributions that you made into Social Security during your working years. That's 15 percent tax-free income. If you can wait for benefits and get a bigger check, then you get 15 percent of that bigger check tax free. As cost-of-living adjustments increase, that tax-free income continues to grow as well.

Third, more survivor benefits. If you have a spouse and your check is the higher one, by deferring to age seventy, that becomes the amount your spouse will receive as a survivor. If you defer your check all the way to age seventy and receive $3,000 a month in Social Security benefits and something happens to you, your survivor gets to keep receiving 100 percent of your $3,000 amount. This is true even if the spouse started his or her own Social Security benefit at age sixty-two, as long as he or she is older than the full retirement age when the survivor benefit starts.

You will always get your Social Security benefit, but if your spouse's record provides more benefit, then you will receive the difference between those amounts, in addition to what you are already receiving. I like to think of that in a different way, to make it simple to understand. Bottom line, you get to keep the higher Social Security amount, while the lower check stops. If my spouse is getting $2,000 a month and I'm receiving $2,500 a month and

I die, then my spouse will get the higher amount of $2,500, and the $2,000 stops.

Social Security is unable to provide a lot of resources in helping you optimize when to start your Social Security. It really is a question of how long you think you are going to live. They are actually taking more than thirteen thousand applications every single day for Social Security benefits. Most of the benefits are elected online at ssa.gov. You no longer receive a lot of guidance on when you should start your benefits due to the volume of applications and the fact that many seasoned social security workers are also retiring.

The right answer really comes down to planning all your retirement income sources and then fitting Social Security into the mix. If you don't think you're going to live a long time and you're in poor health, maybe you would want to start that Social Security early so you don't withdraw from your investments as quickly with the hope that you will leave more of your assets behind for your heirs. It may also allow you to take some stress off your portfolio by starting Social Security early and drawing less from your investments.

Conversely, maybe you do want to spend down some parts of your portfolio and defer that Social Security and get some of the three benefits I explained earlier—more income, more tax-free income, and a higher survivor benefit in the future. Some of my clients have a pension plan that only pays a 50 percent survivor annuity, which is common. This is the default option, so if one spouse passes away, there's a reduction to the income, which may cause an income shortfall.

Another situation may be that you are in poor health and you're not able to get life insurance to fill that gap or it's too expensive to fill that gap. One strategy is to defer the Social Security check longer to help fill that survivor gap or shortfall due to a lack of pension continuation or life insurance.

Social Security Disability

What happens if you become disabled prior to reaching Social Security age? Social Security benefits will actually pay you disability benefits at any age, as long as you qualify. They do have the strictest definition of disability, which means you cannot perform any job that exists anywhere in the country. Unfortunately, almost a third of our population qualifies under that definition for disability benefits. One-third of all workers will become disabled prior to reaching their Social Security age.

Part of the application process is to provide medical records. Social Security will go to your doctors and collect medical records so they can determine whether you qualify for disability benefits. One of the things you can do to speed up the process is to collect those medical records and provide them to Social Security along with your application.

A part of the Social Security Act allows you as a worker to request medical records from your doctors without any cost. So go and collect those medical records, and take them over to the Social Security Administration when you apply for disability benefits, and you can perhaps speed up the process and the chances of approving your case as soon as possible.

There is also legislation that passed called Compassionate Allowances Conditions, which provides a list of ailments or diseases that qualify a person for an expedited process to get approved for disability benefits as fast as administratively possible.

Of course, you don't hope to qualify by having a condition that is on that list, but if you do, it will help you qualify for benefits quickly. Look at that Compassionate Allowances list at https://www.ssa.gov/compassionate allowances/conditions.htm.

Spouse Benefits

Let's say one spouse worked and the other did not have earned income. Both are actually eligible for Social Security benefits. A spouse can draw benefits based on his or her spouse's earnings record, without affecting the other person's Social Security benefit. A spouse's benefit is based on up to 50 percent of the spouse's record at his or her full retirement age. This is probably one of the most missed items because people think, "Oh, I'm eligible for 50 percent of my spouse's record, so my spouse gets $2,000 and I'll get $1,000 when I'm ready to draw Social Security at age sixty-two." You can start benefits at age sixty-two, assuming your spouse is drawing benefits, but you would only be able to receive about 35 to 40 percent of their full retirement benefit, not 50 percent. You must wait until your Full Retirement Age to get 50 percent.

Social Security benefits are based on a lifetime of earnings of your highest thirty-five years. Near-retirees often think that if they stop working a few years before Social Security eligibility, their Social Security benefit will drop significantly. But since it's based on a lifetime of earnings (thirty-five years indexed to inflation), most do not experience a noticeable drop in their benefit by retiring a few years early. This is great news to those targeting an age-sixty retirement.

When to Begin Social Security Benefits

Tom Clark from the Social Security Administration is one of the most published experts in Social Security. If you were to ask him when you should begin your Social Security benefits, he would be quick to answer, "Just tell me the day you're going to die, and I'll tell when you need to start your benefits." This always gets a few laughs from his audience during speaking engagements, but it does strike at the root, as longevity is the most deterministic factor.

It is very common to see calculations of the break-even point on your Social Security benefits. This is the point at which your benefit will be higher if you don't start benefits at sixty-two and skip those checks for four years and then start benefits at sixty-six or your full retirement age (FRA). How long will you live and collect those higher checks to break even and make up for the forty-eight checks that you didn't get to collect for those four years? This usually calculates to about a twelve-year break-even time period, so you usually have to live to age seventy-eight to have collected a cumulative equivalent amount to starting benefits at age sixty-two.

So if you think you're going to live from age sixty-six to at least age seventy-eight, you will have been better off by waiting, because from that point on, you will be receiving a higher amount and therefore be ahead in the total dollar amount you will collect for the rest of your life.

Another way to look at this question is to frame it from a lifestyle perspective, since there's no ribbon, no award, no etching on your tombstone that says, "I broke even on my Social Security benefit." In the end, it doesn't matter whether you break even. What does matter is whether you get the cash flow in the right period to live your best financial life.

Some people plan to travel in their sixties, and they want to start that check early, so it allows them to travel and do the things they want to do in retirement. If they had waited until later to draw benefits, they may have not been able to reach their retirement lifestyle goals. More income later, if you are not healthy enough to travel, may end up causing you to miss out on a decade of travel that you might not get to do later. That's why understanding your full income plan and lifestyle goals are more important than Social Security break-even calculations.

Taxes on Social Security

Not everyone will pay tax on his or her Social Security. It is estimated that about 80 percent of the people who receive Social Security benefits will pay zero tax on their Social Security. That's because they don't have a significant amount of other income sources, which keeps their income level low enough that it doesn't trigger their Social Security to become taxable. For the rest, there's a twenty-line-item calculation on the Social Security Tax Worksheet to determine whether your Social Security is taxable. And it's the traditional half of this number, greater of these numbers, like you would see in a normal tax worksheet. You can get a copy of the worksheet by visiting irs.gov and downloading Publication 915 and then look for the header *Worksheets*.

From a general rule standpoint, if you're single and have over $25,000 in income from other sources, your Social Security will be taxable. If you're married with over $36,000 in income, your Social Security will be taxed. Fifteen percent of your Social Security is nontaxable, so only up to a maximum of 85 percent of your Social Security benefit amount will be taxed.

Of course, that's ordinary income, and your other income sources will determine how much tax and the tax rate you actually pay on your Social Security benefit. Many people argue they have already paid taxes on their Social Security, and that's true. That's the way the Social Security Administration looks at it, which is why 15 percent of it is nontaxable, because that's the return of your contributions into Social Security during your working years, and the rest of it reflects your employer contributions and growth on those Social Security taxes you paid in. So congratulations—15 percent of your check is not taxable.

The Defined Benefit Pension Plan

If you have a pension plan, you are among the few lucky ones. If you have a defined-benefit pension plan, it means there's a formula behind the pension value. The company contributes all the money, and they create a formula to target a certain amount of income for their employees when they retire. Usually, the target age is sixty-five, which is referred to as *normal retirement age*.

Pensions may offer reduced benefits at earlier retirement ages or when you leave the company, but it's contingent upon the pension calculation and summary plan description, which is a document that outlines the rules of the plan. You can request a copy of the document from your benefits director, plan administrator, or human resources department.

Pensions have many forms. The benefit can be in the form of a lump sum or a monthly check. Pensions can provide a monthly income for your lifetime and for your spouse's lifetime as well. Providing benefits for your spouse naturally reduces the amount you will receive during your lifetime.

A pension benefit that provides a lump sum option is interest-rate sensitive, and its value has an inverse relationship to interest rates. So as interest rates go up, pension lump sum values go down and vice versa. This may seem counterintuitive, but you can think of this relationship as the more you can earn on a lump sum of money, the company will need to pay you less of a pension benefit to provide the same economic benefit over your life span. In today's environment, we are currently experiencing some of the lowest interest rates we may ever experience, and we're seeing higher-than-ever lump sum pension payments.

If your company offers you a lump sum, should you take it? It obviously depends upon what you plan to do with the lump sum. If you decide to spend it or pay off the house or do something that uses up a big portion of the principal right away, then that is typically not your best option for a couple of reasons. First, it's all ordinary income tax when you take it out, so the tax payment can be too costly and too early in your retirement. Second, you will have less money to provide income in retirement.

The interest rate calculations per employer vary widely. Verizon, for example, has monthly interest rate changes that affect their pension value, whereas Texas Instruments and Raytheon use annual updates to their pension rates. It is not uncommon for me to see a retiree ready to retire at the end of the year whose retirement date will play a significant role in determining the lump sum value he or she will receive. Even retiring one day later, such as working until January 1 instead of retiring on December 31, may mean a 10 percent difference in the pension amount. When you have a million-dollar pension lump sum, one extra day could cost you $100,000 in retirement dollars. The calculation is complex, so check out whether your employer has a benefit center, or ask a financial planner to help you calculate it.

The key, when you get close to retirement, is to request benefit estimates and start understanding how your pension value changes with various retirement dates and interest rates. Also, run multiple estimates to make sure you're optimizing your pension benefit.

Defined Contribution Plans

If you were starting your own company with several employees and you wanted to set up a pension plan as an incentive for your employees to stay long term, you would find that you would have two broad pension choices: defined-benefit or defined-contribution plans. Defined-benefit pension plans would be a fit if you said, "I want to provide a certain amount of benefits when my employees turn age sixty-five, to benefit them for the rest of their lives." Based on those calculations and potential earnings, you would have to make contributions to an investment account annually that you manage, to provide your employees with the target benefit or income amount at age sixty-five. If your investments performed poorly, you would have to put in more contributions to shore up the difference. With expensive actuarial fees to calculate this every year, you can see how this may be a challenge, which is why we have recently seen more companies move to defined-contribution plans instead of defined-benefit plans.

In contrast, you could set up a defined-contribution plan for your employees, which would require you to contribute a percentage of their compensation annually to their pension plan. In a defined-contribution plan, the employee manages it, so the cost and risk of having to perform more calculations or add additional funds to the plan is eliminated. In essence, you've transferred the risk and responsibility from the employer to the employee to invest those assets for a future retirement benefit. Typically, defined-contribution plan contributions are added to the employee's 401(k) account.

Lump Sum versus Annuity Payment Options

In either case, the employer will usually give you different pension payment options at retirement. If they offer you a lump sum, should you take it? It really depends on several factors, such as your personal goals and circumstances, as well as what the pension plan offers as a benefit. Sometimes companies make it more attractive to take the lump sum, and then of course, there are cases where the annuity is more attractive. So how do you know if it is a good deal? One resource is the *relative value calculation* provided in your pension benefit calculation, which compares all the payment options as a relative value to the single life annuity payment, which pays you an income for the rest of your life but doesn't provide survivor benefits.

You really have to spend some time evaluating the annuity

payment options. What I typically do is take the monthly annuity payment you receive, multiply it by twelve to convert it to an annual benefit amount (ABA), and then divide it by the lump sum (LS) payment option, and that will give you the effective withdrawal rate on the investment. Let's say you have a $300,000 lump sum and the monthly payment of $1,500 as a single life annuity, and we use the formula ABA/LS = withdrawal rate. Then $1,500 x 12 = $18,000 is the ABA. So ABA: 18,000 / LS: 300,000 = 6%. This formula will give you a quick way to evaluate investment options for investing your lump sum by comparing yields. You may be asking, "If I were to invest my lump sum to get a 6 percent payment for the rest of my life, would it be equivalent to my pension annuity offer?" This formula helps answer that question.

One of the reasons most employees tend to opt for a lump sum is not because of the income benefits but because of the survivor benefits. The annuity payment will pay you for as long as you live, or if you have spouse protection, it will provide lifetime benefits for your spouse as well. But if you only receive the first monthly check and both of you are killed in an auto accident, then no payments or benefits would be left to your heirs.

Of course, the lump sum option provides more flexibility than a monthly lifetime payment, and you may also be able to leave the leftover balance for your heirs if properly invested.

Principle 4

Fund the Gap

It takes as much energy to wish as it does to plan.

—Eleanor Roosevelt

The fundamental challenge with retirement is identifying and funding the income gap. First, you need to envision what your retirement lifestyle will look like. How often are you going to travel, and what will your hobbies cost? You can then adjust your estimated expenses to get the best estimate of your retirement lifestyle and how much it will cost.

For you to be able to identify your income gap, you have to review what you've learned in this book so far regarding cash flow, the importance of understanding how much you are taking home and where the money is going. Then understand how much income you'll have from other sources, such as Social Security and pension plans.

Then you look to the other assets you have saved, to start identifying how much more monthly income you're going to need from your investments. Have you saved enough to fill the income gap? Have you saved enough to be unemployed for the next thirty to forty years? You may spend more years in retirement than you did while working.

It can seem daunting at first, but the younger you are when you identify this gap, the more you can be focused on saving the right amount so you're prepared when you make the decision to retire. Most retirees have told me "I wish I had started saving sooner." That's because retirement funding gaps don't close themselves; they take deliberate habits of saving, planning, and investing.

401(k) Pretax—Matching and Contributions

Today, 401(k) plans have become the most widely offered retirement savings account. Typically, it's the number-one way to save for retirement. I usually refer to 401(k) plans as the best place to contribute and save for retirement because of the tax-deferred benefits and matching contributions that you don't get in other investment options.

Now 401(k) plans are even offering Roth contributions, where the money goes in after taxes and then comes out tax free in retirement. Many plans offer different types of contributions into the 401(k) plans and sufficient investment options to diversify your investments.

Inside the 401(k)

A company stock fund is sometimes offered inside the 401(k) if your company is publicly traded. The stock fund does not trade like a stock as you cannot buy and sell it mid-day. Instead it works like a mutual fund, as you get to buy and sell the stock fund at the end of the day. The stock fund is usually comprised of 97% company stock and a 3% cash allocation, but it varies depending on the company and custodian. The stock fund is a method for employees to buy company stock easily.

One of the mistakes a lot people make is concentrating their wealth in the stock for their employer, which comes with a lot of risk. If something happens to the company, they not only lose their job but their 401(k) value that is invested in the company stock. That happened significantly in the dot-com era, when it hit a lot of telecoms, such as MCI and Nortel. People lost their jobs and the full value of their retirement savings.

One person I met with told me about how he had $2 million of Nortel stock that went worthless. Not only that, he had to scramble to get his pension before the company folded. Being aware of not concentrating your wealth all in the company where you work is a fundamental part of increasing your odds of reaching your retirement goals.

After-Tax Contributions

Some legacy 401(k) accounts will allow you to contribute after-tax contributions to the 401(k) above the pretax thresholds of $19,500 or $26,000 if you are over age fifty. Making an after-tax contribution is almost like a tax loophole; it is kind of like getting your cake and eating it too. You can put it in after-tax dollars, the money grows, and all the growth will come back to you as pretax dollars in the future. But in the meantime, you can actually withdraw all those after-tax dollars you contributed, without any tax consequences. For example, if you were able to save $50,000 in after-tax contributions, when you retire, you will get a $50,000 check without any taxes owed.

If your employer offers that, it's a good way of adding some additional flexibility and dollars that you'll get right at retirement.

401(k) Loans

Have you heard the myth, "I'm going to borrow money from my 401(k) because I'm just going to pay myself back and that's better than paying the bank interest"? The idea that 401(k) loans (as many refer to the process, "borrowing from yourself") is a better financing choice is really just a myth. Imagine you were told that the bank was offering a loan that would be based on stock market returns that year, meaning that your interest rate might be 18 percent or 33 percent if the market did well. However, if the market did poorly, then you would have a very low rate. Nobody would sign up for that loan because of the risk that they might end up paying too high of an interest rate. But in fact, when you're taking a 401(k) loan, you're really signing up for the same thing. You are selling shares out of your account today to get the money, and when you pay it back, your investment has potentially gone up in value, so you're buying back those same shares at higher prices. You do not end up with the same number of shares when you buy it back. It could end up costing you a pretty significant amount.

The other issue with 401(k) loans is double taxation. When you're putting money back in, as you repay the loan with after-tax dollars, then when you take that money out in retirement, it is all taxable. The interest you're paying on the 401(k) loan is getting double taxed.

A 401(k) loan is usually what I recommend as a last resort for where to get funds, especially in the strong stock market and low-interest-rate environments we have today.

Retirement Is All about Cash Flow

Many retirees face a lot of different trade-offs when they retire. How do you choose across those trade-offs, making sure you can afford to replace the paycheck and afford to retire? The number-one question seems to be "Should I pay off my mortgage and my debts at retirement?"

Usually the answer is "Yes, if it will increase overall cash flow." It is no longer about accumulation and leverage, like it is when you began saving for retirement. At retirement, the decision is about reducing your cash outflow and increasing your cash inflow.

You may say, "I want to pay off my mortgage, and I still owe $100,000 on my mortgage," and you have to take it from pretax funds. That usually doesn't make sense, because you'll easily pay over 24 percent in taxes all at once. If you take $100,000 out, you will need to have $131,578.95 to pay off the $100,000 balance if you're in the 24 percent bracket.

So $31,578.95 goes to Uncle Sam up front, and that usually is not a good thing. But if you have other assets you can use to pay off the mortgage, then it's usually an efficient thing to do. If you look at it from an effective withdrawal rate, the same way you looked at it earlier, you can take the mortgage times twelve and say this is the mortgage payment that is going away, and this is the balance I'm paying.

Usually, you may get an 8 percent, 10 percent, or even a 12 percent yield by paying off debts. If you're not going to get that on investing that money, then it makes sense to pay off the debts to increase cash flow for retirement. If cash flow goes up by paying down those debts immediately and it doesn't require a big tax bill or too much of your assets, then I typically recommend it.

Living Longer

We've all heard that one of the risks of a retirement plan is you will live longer, and your money will have to support you for more years than your parents, but how much longer?

Longevity improves by about one year per decade, today's thirty-five-year-olds could expect to live three years longer than today's sixty-five-year-olds.

Longevityillustrator.org is from the Society of Actuaries and the American Academy of Actuaries. It provides longevity estimates based upon gender, age, smoking status, and overall health. (Pfau 2017)

Health Insurance Reduces Cash Flow

By far the number-one concern of near-retirees is whether they will be able to retire, due to the cost of having an affordable health care option. For retirees over the age of sixty-five, Medicare will be their primary insurance.

Medicare

Almost everybody has heard of Medicare, but many people don't understand the basics. Medicare has different parts: Part A, Part B, Part C, and Part D.

Part A is hospitalization, and that's the part of Medicare you pay for while you are working, so once you retire, there's no premium. People say Medicare Part A is free in retirement, but I like to say it's prepaid, rather than free.

Part B acts as traditional insurance, your 80/20 plan. Medicare pays 80 percent of your costs and doctors' visits in retirement; 20 percent you are responsible for. Many people have had $2 million medical bills, and some say, "Great news; you have Medicare, and 80 percent is covered." The bad news is that 20 percent is not covered, so that's $400,000 you're going to have to pay for the coverage. If Medicare is your primary insurance, then you should sign up for Part B without exception.

That's where Medigap or Gap Plans come into play. A Medigap plan is like additional insurance you can buy to cover the 20 percent for you, so you're not responsible for that portion. The biggest mistake you can make is not to sign up for Part B, because Part B becomes your primary insurance at age sixty-five, regardless of when you were born. Even if you are military and on Tricare, Medicare pays first at age sixty-five, but there's an exception.

The one exception is if you're actively working and employed by an employer with twenty-five or more employees and covered under that employer's plan or your spouse's active employer plan. In this case, you don't need to sign up for Medicare at age sixty-five, as the employer plan will be your primary insurance. You can defer and then show proof of existing coverage or evidence of coverage (EOC) and sign up later without any type of penalty. The EOC form is signed by your employer and provided to Medicare.

If you forgo Part B and realize your mistake and want to a get it, you can, but you have to wait until the next enrollment period, which is January to March of the following year, but your coverage does not become effective until July. Hopefully, you're not trying to add it because you're sick and you need the coverage at that time. Just note that when you add it back, the premiums will be 10 percent higher for each year you didn't sign up for it after age sixty-five, for the rest of your life.

Part D is for prescription drugs. Part D plans vary widely across different states. The best tool is to go to the medicare.gov website and use their plan finder. You can plug in the prescriptions you're taking, and it will optimize the plan for you. It will also identify the least amount of out-of-pocket based on current prescriptions. Prescriptions change often, so during open enrollment at the end of each year, you can use the plan finder again and change your Part D plan to be the one in which you pay the least amount of out-of-pocket expenses.

It's important for each individual to run the optimizer each year, to find the least expensive Part D plan. Sometimes I see spouses use the same Part D plan, but chances are the spouses are taking different prescriptions and would benefit from having two different Part D plans to minimize their costs.

Medicare Gap Plans

These plans cover the 20 percent portion that you want an insurance company to pay instead of your having to pay it. Minimizing costs works similarly to choosing a Plan D plan. You can use the plan finder on medicare.gov to help you find the Medigap plan with the lowest premium.

Medigap plans are confusing because just like Medicare Parts A, B, C and D, the Medigap plans are also labeled A, B, C, all the way through N. Many people get that confused and wonder, "Is that Part B Medicare or Plan B Medigap?" This is different—a Medigap Plan B is the 20 percent insurance, and the Medicare Part B is the 80 percent insurance.

Typically, Plan G is considered the "Cadillac plan," and right now, the cost is around $150 a month for that coverage. The cost of Medicare Part B is $135.50.

If your yearly income in 2017 (for what you pay in 2019) was			You pay each month (in 2019)
File individual tax return	File joint tax return	File married & separate tax return	
$85,000 or less	$170,000 or less	$85,000 or less	$135.50
above $85,000 up to $107,000	above $170,000 up to $214,000	Not applicable	$189.60
above $107,000 up to $133,500	above $214,000 up to $267,000	Not applicable	$270.90
above $133,500 up to $160,000	above $267,000 up to $320,000	Not applicable	$352.20
above $160,000 and less than $500,000	above $320,000 and less than $750,000	above $85,000 and less than $415,000	$433.40
$500,000 or above	$750,000 and above	$415,000 and above	$460.50

Chart Source: https://www.medicare.gov/your-medicare-costs/part-b-costs

Medicare Part C is the managed-care option or Medicare Advantage. It's something you can sign up for, and there are different providers. It acts as Parts A, B, and D and Medigap all combined into one. It is one premium, typically a lower premium. You need to do your homework, as sometimes you do not get the same quality of benefits or service.

All prices are regulated and set to be fair, so it's slightly different in premiums, and you really have to do your research on which providers are better. They get to collect the insurance premiums from the government, and then, the less they pay out, the more profits they make. Therefore, people like it because it can be a lower cost. Some people do not like it, because they don't feel like they get the same standard of care they want and it may not provide the same coverage while traveling out of state.

Retiree Medical Insurance

If you're retiring before the age of sixty-five, some employers do offer retiree medical insurance to get you to age sixty-five. Those benefits are quickly becoming more expensive and going away, and with the implementation of Obamacare, many people are choosing that option. Under the Affordable Care Act, you can go to healthcare.gov and get a quote on what the insurance would run and compare that to your retiree medical option.

Consolidated Omnibus Budget Reconciliation Act (COBRA)

COBRA coverage will provide you with health insurance benefits for a specified period of time. It allows you to keep your employer insurance plan after you have left the company. If you separated because of a termination or retirement, you are eligible for eighteen months of coverage but will have to pay for 100 percent of the cost, as well as a 3 percent administrative fee. Coverage can last longer if you are leaving employment because of a disability. There's a five-month extension that will bridge you into getting onto Medicare because Medicare has a twenty-four-month waiting period. You need to elect COBRA coverage within sixty days of leaving your current employment.

I recommend you begin spending some time on the Medicare website, medicare.gov, so you can begin understanding your options. As overwhelming as it may appear at first, a little research and planning will help you feel more comfortable with your health care options and make an earlier retirement a possibility.

Principle 5

Climbing Mount Everest

> Courage is being scared to death but saddling up anyway.
>
> —John Wayne

Every year, climbers go out to the base of Mount Everest with one goal. Do you know what it is? Get to the top, right? Well, I'm going to argue that the real goal is to get down the other side of the mountain and live to tell the story—and maybe even post some pictures on Facebook.

Retirement planning is like climbing Mount Everest. What is the goal? Everybody seems to focus on getting to retirement, but I claim the real goal is to get through retirement and not run out of money.

The Same Accumulation Strategies Won't Work in Retirement

Getting up the mountain and down the mountain are significantly different. Investors spend time accumulating assets, and they train themselves on what it takes to be successful to get to retirement. They focus on things like saving consistently, dollar-cost averaging (contributing the same dollar regardless of share prices), and buying and holding long term.

Wade Pfau states,

> They realize that if they do those things, they will get the average return. But in retirement, they try to apply those same concepts and the problem arises if they run into a market loss early in their retirement and they're drawing money out for income. They can very quickly run out of money, even though their long-term average return was just fine. A key lesson for long-term financial planning is that you should not expect to earn the average historical market returns for your portfolio. Half the time, realized returns will be less ... Dismiss any retirement projection based on 8 or 12 percent returns, as the reality is likely much less when we account for portfolio volatility, inflations, and

a desire to develop a plan that will work more than half the time and in today's low interest rates. (2017)

I like to refer to what I have begun calling the "default retirement plan," as I've heard people explain their plan for retirement to me so many times. Here is how it usually goes: "I can earn 8 percent on my money. I found a mutual fund that has been around since the 1960s, with a great track history, and it has always averaged 8 percent. I've calculated I can live on 5 percent of my money, so I'm going to be earning 8 percent and only spend 5 percent. Therefore, I should have 3 percent left over for inflation." Do you think their plan has any risk of running out of money?

The answer is yes, because they won't earn 8 percent every year; that's just the average. Some years will have great returns, and some years the annual returns will be negative. If you retired in the peak of 2007 and experienced the downturn in 2008 and 2009 and drew out 5 percent from your portfolio, then you could get so far behind that you may never recover. Therefore, even if your portfolio averages 8 percent over the long term and you spend less than the average earnings, you may still run out of money. What can happen is that you may sell too many shares early on as you have to sell more shares to receive the same income because the market value of each share drops.

This risk we are referring to is called "sequence-of-returns risk." As Pfau (2017) explains, "Sequence-of-returns risk is amplified by greater portfolio volatility, yet many retirees cannot afford to play it too safe. Short-term fixed-income securities might struggle to provide returns that exceed inflation, causing these assets to be quite risky in a different sense: they may not be able to support a retiree's long-term spending goals."

Taking distributions amplifies investment risks (market volatility, interest-rate volatility, and credit risk) by increasing the importance of the order of investment returns in retirement.

Building a retirement income strategy is a process that requires determining how to best combine available retirement income tools, in order to meet retirement goals and to effectively protect against the risks standing in the way of those goals.

The most efficient retirement strategies require an integration of both investments and insurance. It is potentially harmful to dismiss subsets of retirement income tolls without a thorough investigation of their purported role. In this regard, describe the stock market as a casino, to lump income annuities together with every other type of annuity, and to dismiss reverse mortgages without any further consideration. (Pfau 2017)

Distribution Planning Impact

Your investment choices and how you make decisions will be directly related to the degree to which you compensate for sequence-of-returns risk in your retirement portfolio and cash-flow plan. People underestimate the long-term impact of what happens during market declines until it is too late. After all, you have probably always heard that you should not panic but rather buy and hold your investments for the long term. However, while you wait for markets to make a comeback, your spending needs for the portfolio don't automatically decrease. In Wade Pfau's book (2017), he states, "To put it succinctly, retirees experience reduced capacity to bear financial market risk once they have retired." This is because what you actually experience is quite different when you're in retirement, since the emotional aspect and responsibility as an investor is heightened and amplified. You are now dependent upon your portfolio cash flows for your livelihood.

Let's examine what happens if you're watching your portfolio value drop in your first year in retirement and you are drawing out 5 percent for income. Let's say you started with a $1 million portfolio, meaning you're taking out $50,000 for income this year, but the portfolio drops 15 percent. Do you have the investor fortitude (the stomach) to do the right thing and let the value recover? Many people don't, and they sell their investments too quickly, as they tend to conclude that if losses continue at the same rate, they will soon run out of money. Markets don't ever continue on the same path at the same rate. Why do investors commonly make this mistake? The root is derived from the human ability for pattern recognition, which is formidable, as recognizing patterns allows us to predict and expect what is coming. (Klaff 2011) However, it also supports a tendency to quickly build conclusions on current patterns and makes it very difficult to not panic and react by doing all the wrong things when it comes to investing.

It's almost impossible as a retirement investor to be really prepared for such a decline in your portfolio, which is why the first downturn in retirement usually shakes retirees. There are some strategies we will talk about later that can help you avoid these unfortunate experiences.

The reality is that the timing of failure, post-career, increases the risk. The American College Professor, Wade D. Pfau, states,

> Retirement individual investors are extremely vulnerable to the sequence of market returns experienced

over their investing lifetimes. Individuals, who behave exactly the same over their careers, saving the same percentage of the same salary for the same number of years, can otherwise experience very different outcomes based solely upon the specific sequence of investment returns, which accompanies their career and retirement. The vulnerability reaches its peak at the retirement date, as this is the point in which a return to employment becomes increasingly difficult and a post-retirement market drop can be devastating. Actual wealth accumulations and sustainable withdrawal rates will vary substantially for different retirees, as these outcomes depend disproportionately on the shorter sequence of returns just before and after the retirement date. (2013)

Let's face it: retiring in the right year with the right sequence of future returns is not something you can control. The good news is that you can structure your investment portfolio to accommodate such risk and reduce the impact that these sequences will have in determining your success in retirement.

Cash Flow Is More Important Than Interest Rate Savings

It is easy to focus on the fact that you may be able to earn more in investing than in paying off your debts, thinking you can earn more than the interest rates you are paying. For example, if your interest rate is only 3 percent, then perhaps you can earn more in the market, so why worry about paying off debt? However, you may also have to endure a lengthy time period when you will not have the disposable income required to get to travel, and check off the bucket list items that you hoped to do in retirement. That's because in retirement, what really matters is getting your income above your expenses. The cost of paying interest out of your investments creates more strain and more income requirements on your investments, which can cause you to run out of money earlier.

The result of this phenomenon is that to be successful, you must approach retirement income planning with a different mindset. Your financial success is no longer about accumulating assets, but rather about having more cash flow. This means you have to shift your mind-set or paradigm from accumulation to distribution. Stress test the portfolio and your investment plan to confirm it is aligned with how to get through retirement (down the mountain)—not just how to get *to* retirement (up the mountain). Then the search for an investment model that can help you navigate and manage these risks begins. The Financial Planning Association (FPA), of which I am a member, divides retirement income strategies into three categories: time-based segmentation, systematic withdrawals, and essential-versus-discretionary income, which are what you will learn about in the next chapter.

Time-Based Segmentation

Years back, there was big talk about having buckets of money. The strategy required that you invest a portion of your money for the first ten years in retirement and then another portion for the next ten years (years ten through twenty), and then the final portion of your money for years twenty and on. The plan was to spend down the first bucket, and by the time that's gone, the next bucket should have already performed well enough to replace the first bucket, plus inflation.

Unfortunately, for retirees who adopted this model, those strategies did not fare well during the 2001 and 2008 market downturns, as they did not adequately account for the sequence-of-returns risk. Unfortunately, many who used those strategies ran out of money. In fact, a lot of the advisers who were recommending them ended up with lawsuits due to the financial ruin they created for their clients.

The bucket strategy does not work consistently because it requires too much from your assets in the first ten years, and if the market cycle does not cooperate, it results in a short-lived retirement portfolio. Therefore, you're better off starting with a strong baseline of income (lifetime income) and then, depending on the rest of the assets, only adding income over the long term as necessary for inflation.

Systematic Withdrawals

This is the most common type of plan, and in fact, I like to refer to it as the "default strategy" because I hear about it so much. It's the all-in method.

Here is how it goes: you add up your total assets, pick a withdrawal rate, such as 3 to 4 percent of the starting value at retirement, to be conservative on how much you draw out, and hope you earn more than you spend. Unfortunately, this strategy falls subject to that sequence-of-returns risk and can be difficult to hold true to the strategy during market drops.

Importance of Separating Income and Growth Assets

So how do you avoid the sequence-of-returns risk in retirement? What I recommend is to always have two types of investments, one investment for income and another for growth. By isolating income assets, you're able to focus on cash-flow investments or investments that provide predictable cash flow regardless of market conditions. In this way, you avoid the need to draw out money immediately from your growth investments and provide more time for the value to double. Since you're not selling shares when the markets are down, they don't fall subject to the sequence-of-returns risk.

Should I Use Pretax or After-Tax Money for My Income Plan?

Many advisers and retirement models will show distributions from your after-tax assets first and then later, distributions from your pretax assets. For example, you would be spending down your savings and nonqualified investment accounts, while continuing to defer your 401(k) and IRAs, until you have to start taking distributions at age 70 1/2 to meet required minimum distributions that the IRS requires.

Waiting until later to begin distribution on your pretax investments may cause you to pay more in taxes overall during your retirement. If you have positioned your after-tax assets to provide a predictable income stream during retirement and then have to begin taking from your pretax investments at age 70 1/2, you will potentially jump your income to the next tax bracket, which you cannot get out of, unless you redo your investment strategy. Many times, movements to restructure your investment strategy cause taxation, so it may result in a tax problem you can't affordably get out of. Therefore, I advise my clients to start with their qualified assets for distributions after age 59½ to pay tax in the lowest bracket possible. Deferring everything else gives them more flexibility during retirement and helps reduce the amount of required minimum distributions they will have to take in retirement. Required minimum distributions will be about 3.65 percent of all of your pretax investments at age 70 1/2. By beginning distributions years before, you may limit the required amount you have to take out and provide yourself with more control and flexibility over your tax bill. Otherwise, you may end up with a much larger pretax portfolio, which pushes you into a higher tax bracket that you can never get out of without paying even more tax.

Sustainable Withdrawal Rates

The sustainability of your retirement portfolio and income will depend on your withdrawal rate, your investment yield, and your longevity. Obviously, the lower the withdrawal rate, the longer your money will last. Therefore, being realistic with your withdrawal rate at retirement is one of the first decisions you will need to make. Determining your withdrawal rate is also one of the most important factors to focus on, since you have the most control over it.

Monte Carlo Simulation

Too many financial models assume a set percentage of return with a steady withdrawal rate which predicts about how long the money will last without giving any value to the fact that markets don't give a specified rate of return each year. Market returns fluctuate widely; therefore, better models are required to account for this variance or uncertainty factor. One such tool is the Monte Carlo Simulation, which utilizes historical returns and repeats them in different sequences thousands of times, which provides a percentage to illustrate the probability of success. If you are 85 percent confident you will not run out of money in retirement, is that good enough? My thoughts are that if you were boarding an airplane and there was an illuminated sign stating, "You have an 85 percent probability that the airplane will make it to its destination," you wouldn't board the plane. Retirement income plans require a great deal of certainty, so how will you find a plan that you understand and feel confident that it will work for you in retirement? Statistical calculations of confidence are good starting points to gain a greater understanding, but they don't go far enough in explaining how to formulate an action plan and providing the level of confidence you need to live your best financial life without the worry of running out.

You have to create a real strategy that works in all market conditions. You need to feel 100 percent sure you're not going to run out of money. The Monte Carlo simulations do a poor job of predicting your particular experience and the retirement results you will have, as they just give you a range of possible experiences. Which experience you will have cannot be determined by the model.

Sources of Lifetime Income

Another way to eliminate the sequence-of-returns risk is to take some of your money and purchase an annuity to provide a lifetime of income payments. Then, what you've done is shift the risk from yourself and your investments to an insurance company. How much risk is worth transferring?

I recommend the amount you protect be the amount you will need to use for income, to cover your basic needs or the amount you must have each month, no matter what. After examining your current sources of lifetime income, you will be able to determine if you are still short of your income goal. You can then transfer a portion of your retirement savings to close that gap. It is like buying a personal pension plan. Then, once you have enough lifetime income for your basic needs, you can sleep a lot better, knowing that you won't be in a situation that will require you to go back to work.

In summary, understanding the difference between accumulation and distribution and how those differences impact your retirement will help you know how to structure your investments for success. Failure is not an option in retirement. Similar to retirement, most fatalities on Mount Everest happen on the way down, due to a lack of planning for the unexpected and not bringing enough oxygen for the trip down because they were so busy planning for how they would get to the top. Building the right retirement strategy can help you plan how you will successfully navigate the unexpected and make it through retirement without running out of money.

Principle 6

One Shot to Get It Right

> There are constants in life ... change, choice, and principles.
>
> —Stephen Covey

Income Strategies

Although there are several ways to structure a retirement income strategy, the fundamental approaches can be narrowed down to three. Optimizing and running your income strategy efficiently over time requires diligence to make the adjustments needed as the environment changes. Pfau states, "The challenge of retirement income plans is the balance of lifestyle, legacy, longevity, and liquidity" (2017). Let's now examine the last of the three income strategies.

Essential versus Discretionary Income

Retirement is a once-in-a-lifetime event, even if you have worked several jobs and retired and gone back to work. At the end of the day, retirement means you no longer are working for monetary purposes. You have to live on what you have saved, and you have one shot to structure that plan and get it right. The wrong plan can mean that you end up working for the rest of your life, trying to recover from a bad decision. Succinctly stated:

> A retirement income plan should be based on planning to live, not planning to die.
>
> Investing in retirement is not to maximize risk-adjusted returns, but first to ensure that basics will be covered in any market environment and then to invest for additional upside.
>
> The idea is to first build a floor of very low-risk guaranteed income sources to serve your basic spending needs in retirement.
>
> The general view of safety-first advocates is that there is no such thing as a safe withdrawal rate from a volatile portfolio. A truly safe withdrawal rate is unknown and unknowable. Retirees only receive an opportunity to obtain sustainable cash flows from their savings and must develop a strategy that will meet basic needs no matter the length of life or the sequence of postretirement market returns and inflation. Retirees have little leeway for error, as returning to the labor force might not be a realistic option. (Pfau 2017)

The Solution: The Quadrant Strategy

I have outlined the risk that sequence-of-returns presents in retirement, so what is the solution? The solution is the "Quadrants of Retirement," as there are four components of every financial plan for retirement. The four components are designed to structure your assets in these four categories for your plan to be sustainable and potentially weather any market downturn.

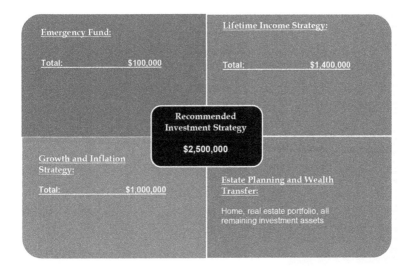

Quadrant 1—The Emergency Fund

These are assets you can access anytime you need them. These assets are liquid and available to you. Typically, it's no more than 10 percent of your net worth in that quadrant.

Quadrant 2—Lifetime Income Sources

Pensions, Social Security, and a portion of your investments that will help you meet your basic needs in retirement will be based upon the withdrawal rate you choose. If you use 4 percent in this model, you can shift assets into that quadrant that will provide the retirement income sufficient to meet your essential needs.

Quadrant 3—The Growth and Inflation Assets

These are assets that you're going to invest in for the long term. You're probably not going to touch them the first ten years of retirement. Those assets should have a target growth rate to meet your objectives. Typically, I aim for a 7 percent growth rate, which means the asset should double in ten years.

This is the whole key to flexibility in your plan and in making sure your plan is sustainable. I recommend 30 percent of your portfolio at a minimum in the growth component. Sometimes people are ready to retire, have an emergency fund, and have enough income, but only 10 percent of their net worth is in growth.

That's a red flag that your plan may not be sustainable over the long term and may not keep up with the inflation rate. So a good target is to have 30 percent or more in the growth quadrant, which will give you more confidence that you can sustain a 4 percent inflation rate and have your financial plan much more flexible and sustainable throughout retirement.

The reason the growth investment works by just putting in 30 percent of the portfolio is that you have funded the income plan, which aims to provide sufficient time for the growth portfolio to double during the first ten years of retirement. If you start with $1 million in the growth investment, it works to become $2 million ten years later. You can then take all the growth of $1 million out, shift that to quadrant 2, and create more income for retirement, and allow that remaining $1 million in the growth quadrant to double again over the next decade so you can move half again to the income portfolio.

Another thing that many people don't factor in is that you're ten years older. So as you start shifting to the retirement income quadrant, you can obtain more income. Even if you're buying an annuity, you're ten years older, and your life expectancy is shorter. If you're age sixty, you may only be able to obtain a 4 to 5 percent withdrawal rate. If you're age seventy, you're looking at 5 to 6 percent. If you're age eighty, you're looking at 6 to 8 percent for dollars invested.

Therefore, even the same $1 million you keep moving from your growth investments to your income investments may provide exponential compounding income for inflation protection. As you can see, the key is to start out your retirement with enough in the growth quadrant.

Clients who are very comfortable and have very little concern for long-term inflation usually have 40 to 50 percent in their growth assets compared to their retirement income bucket. Those are my clients who travel the world and don't worry about cash flow in retirement. Whereas allowing your growth assets to fall below the 20 percent threshold may put your long-term income plan at risk due to not adequately protecting against inflation.

Quadrant 4—Estate Planning

Estate planning is about the assets you want to leave behind. Some people want to leave charities large sums of funds, while others want to leave money to their children. Most folks say, "You know, I plan to spend everything but whatever is left, they can have." I've met a select few who say, "I want to spend every penny and let the last check to the undertaker bounce!"

Quadrant Strategy

In looking at the quadrants, it's important you get the right quantity of assets in each box. But it's also important to think through your plan and identify which types of investments should be in each quadrant. For your emergency fund, it makes sense to invest in cash equivalents such as checking accounts, savings accounts, money markets, and cash deposits. In the income portfolio, you might use a mixture of annuities or fixed investments or real estate that provide guaranteed cash flow.

Then, in the growth quadrant, you're looking for stocks, mutual funds, and market-based investments that have higher long-term growth rates and have some liquidity. That way, even if you spend down your emergency fund, you can shift assets from growth to replace the emergency fund over time. Look for things that are liquid and flexible but have higher growth rates.

The estate-planning assets, like life insurance, are typically assets that can be there to help maximize what is left behind. More on maximizing your estate when we get to principal eight.

The other thing the quadrants will do for you is help you visualize your retirement plan and understand the mechanism of how you're going to keep pace with inflation. The ability to visualize and understand your long-term cash flow and investment plan will provide you with more confidence than any spreadsheet ever could.

Why Invest in Two Strategies

Why does investing in two strategies work versus just having all those assets in one bucket? The reason is, if you were to have significant market downturns, the income assets are guaranteed, protected, conservative assets. The growth investments can fluctuate in the market, and you're not planning to use those for ten years. It helps you avoid the sequence-of-returns risk we discussed earlier. It is also about optimizing your overall strategy, but how do you know when it is optimal? The strategy will balance total lifetime spending while maximizing the assets remaining compared to another strategy.

Why After-Tax Assets Should Be Positioned for Growth Rather Than Income

It is a good idea to put assets in the growth quadrant that are after-tax so you're not forced to take them out at age 70 1/2. I found that positioning after-tax assets for growth provides more flexibility than pretax investments such as IRAs.

How to Draw Up Your Own Plan

Creating a projected retirement income and tax analysis can start with outlining your plan with your current income. Look at your take-home pay, and get a monthly total. Next, review your retirement income sources, such as Social Security, pensions, rental income, and all other sources of income besides investments. Then, determine your monthly expenses or use the same value as your current net income if you feel like you are spending what you make but not more.

Finally, identify the monthly income gap or the difference between your current net income and expenses and the retirement income you are able to generate. You can then use your retirement investments to fill that gap by using no more than 60 percent of your retirement assets in the income quadrant. Based on that, calculate the withdrawal rate of 5 percent and how much that will give you. The remaining investments can be used for long-term growth and inflation and should be no less than 30 percent of your total investments. Remember, you need 5 to 10 percent of your investments in the emergency fund category.

You'll then arrive at the amount of income you'll have before taxes, and you can use any tax calculator online or visit SaturdayEveryday.com to review a tax summary to determine your net income amount. Now you get to see if that meets your income and lifestyle goals in retirement. If it doesn't, you know you'll need to run a tighter budget and save more to close the gap. The earlier you do this calculation, the easier it will be to make the necessary changes.

INCOME SOURCES*	CURRENT NET INCOME	RETIRED AGE 65
WORKING INCOME	$ 115,000	
RETIREMENT INCOME		
PENSION 100% JOINT		$ 30,000
IRA INVESTMENTS $1,400,000 (CLOSES THE GAP)		$ 70,000
SOCIAL SECURITY INCOME		$ 31,200
GROWTH ASSETS		
IRA INVESTMENTS $500,000		
AFTER-TAX INVESTMENTS $500,000		
EMERGENCY FUND		
SAVINGS $100,000		
TOTAL INCOME	$ 115,000	$ 131,200
TAX ANALYSIS		
TAXABLE INCOME		$ 100,820
TOTAL TAX		$13,897
EFFECTIVE TAX RATE		10.59%
NET MONTHLY INCOME	**$ 9,583**	**$ 9,775**
LIVING EXPENSES	$ 9,000	$ 9,000
SURPLUS / (DEFICIT)	$ 583	$ 775

Principle 7

A Bucket of Taxes

> Not everything that can be counted counts, and not everything that counts can be counted.
>
> —Albert Einstein

The Tax Bucket

As the adage goes, "It's not how much you make but how much you get to keep." Tax planning is your biggest opportunity in retirement planning, as the less tax you pay, the more you get to spend during retirement. You will most likely spend your entire working career investing in a way that defers paying taxes on your savings for retirement. Therefore, it's powerful to set up a distribution plan that optimizes the taxes on those distributions on an annual basis. Therefore, spending time with your tax adviser to review distribution strategies that enable you to yield more out of your retirement savings will be time well spent.

Sometimes, however, it is easy to fall into the rut of not thinking correctly about the way taxes work. Too many times, we catch ourselves evaluating how we do on taxes by whether we will receive a refund. It is easy to look at it this way, even though you know what really matters is how much you pay in total taxes.

In case you have fallen into the trap of thinking of taxes this way, it may help to start viewing taxes differently. I want you to think of taxes as a bucket that you put money into throughout the year. One way you put money into the tax bucket is through your federal withholding from your paychecks. At the end of the year, you reconcile on the tax return and say, "Well, did I give them too much money, or do I still owe them money?" Once you have that settled, you can get money back out of that bucket, a refund. Or you may owe taxes at the end because you didn't put enough money into the bucket during the year. How much you owe or how much you get back isn't as important as the total amount you had to put into the tax bucket, your total tax. Think about your tax return last year, can you remember your total tax or just your refund amount or perhaps the amount you still owed?

The more you plan and optimize your retirement distributions, the less money you need to put into the tax bucket, which means you'll have more to spend in retirement.

If Taxable Income is:

Over	But Not Over	The Tax Is	Am't Over
Married Filing Jointly and Surviving Spouse			
$0	$19,400	$0+10%	$0
19,400	78,950	$1,940+12%	19,400
78,950	168,400	$9,086+22%	78,950
168,400	321,450	$28,765+24%	168,400
321,450	408,200	$65,497+32%	321,450
408,200	612,350	$93,257+35%	408,200
612,350		$164,709.50+37%	612,350
Single			
$0	$9,700	$0+10%	$0
9,700	39,475	970+12%	9,700
39,475	84,200	4,543+22%	39,475
84,200	160,725	14,382.50+24%	84,200
160,725	204,100	32,748.50+32%	160,725
204,100	510,300	46,628.50+35%	204,100
510,300		153,798.50+37%	510,300
Married Filing Separately			
$0	$9,700	$0+10%	$0
9,700	39,475	970+12%	9,700
39,475	84,200	4,543+22%	39,475
84,200	160,725	14,382.50+24%	84,200
160,725	204,100	32,748.50+32%	160,725
204,100	306,175	46,628.50+35%	204,100
306,175		82,354.75+37%	306,175
Head of Household			
$0	$13,850	$0+10%	$0
13,850	52,850	1,385+12%	13,850
52,850	84,200	6,065+22%	52,850
84,200	160,700	12,962+24%	84,200
160,700	204,100	31,322+32%	160,700
204,100	510,300	45,210+35%	204,100
510,300		152,380+37%	510,300
Estates & Trusts			
$0	$2,600	$0+10%	$0
2,600	9,300	260+24%	2,600
9,300	12,750	1,868+35%	9,300
12,750		3,075.50+37%	12,750

Age Rules

There are a lot of age rules about retirement assets. Since you get to defer assets, the IRS gets to dictate when you get access to those assets. If you draw the money too early or too late, there can be penalties involved.

Retiring Too Early

If you want to retire and access any of your pretax money prior to age 59½, the IRS limits what you can draw out—or you have an *early distribution penalty*, which is 10 percent on all assets that you withdraw from your pretax money IRAs, 401(k)s and other tax-deferred investments. So how do people retire before 59½? There are a couple of loopholes. You can do what is called a *72(t) distribution*, which is the IRS code for signing up for a periodic payment without the 10 percent penalty. This means you have to draw out a periodic payment based on your lifetime. Many people will choose to sign up for a monthly check, and if you go this route, you have to draw that same check amount without changing it for a minimum of five years or until you are 59½, whichever is longer.

If you start at age 50, you have to take that same payment from that IRA or from the pretax money, all the way until 59½ without changing it. If you decide to change the amount, decrease it or increase it, you would have to pay a 10 percent penalty on everything you have drawn out so far. Once you sign up for that 72(t) distribution, you can't get out of it, and you have to stick with it. It's a pretty steep penalty for early retirement.

However, it allows you to draw money from your IRA consistently and early while avoiding that IRS 10 percent penalty. Also, if you're disabled, that 10 percent penalty doesn't apply. There are only a few exceptions, such as death, disability, 72(t) distribution, and that's about it. There's not a whole lot of access to tax deferred savings before 59½.

There's also one other special rule we will call the "one-time penalty-free distribution" or now commonly referred to as "the 55 Rule." This means that if you're between ages 55 and 59½ and you have left the company after the age of 55, before the time you roll over your employer assets, you can do a one-time penalty-free distribution of any amount and not pay the 10 percent early distribution penalty—but note that the distribution is taxable as ordinary income.

If you were to take $100,000 distribution out of your 401(k), good news—no 10 percent penalty, but you have $100,000 that shows up on top of the tax return for the year. This is a great way for some people to get out a few years earlier, maybe at age 58, instead of age 59½. You can take out that distribution and retire at the end of the year. Then, in January, you no longer have a paycheck, so you take out a distribution for the whole year that can bridge you until you turn 59½ and can access your other money.

That one-time distribution availability in some retirement accounts depends on your employer, but many plans are written so that they allow you to take an annual distribution rather than just one time. They call it "one time," as long as you have not rolled over the assets. Then you still meet that requirement, and you can do that as an annual distribution. It's another way you can get out a few years early before 59 1/2 and still access your qualified pretax money. It is important to note that early distributions exceptions differ between IRAs and 401(k)s.

Retiring Too Late

If you're working past age 70 1/2, you don't have to take required minimum distributions out of your employer-sponsored plans. But if you have an IRA, the IRS requires that you begin distributions in the amount of at least 3.65 percent of your total IRAs. For example, if you have a $1 million IRA, that's $36,500 you have to draw out and pay tax on. If you don't, it's a significant IRS penalty of 50 percent of what you should have taken, or $18,250 in this case.

You want to make sure you meet that requirement every year, and it's the reason most retirees begin to consolidate their assets and advisers in retirement. It's not uncommon for somebody to work with multiple financial firms as they are accumulating assets. But in retirement, they tend to consolidate to one adviser, so they don't miss required minimum distributions they should have known about.

The distribution you have to take out is based on your December 31 value the prior year, and you have to take the amount out by the end of the year. The first year you turn 70 1/2, you can defer taking that distribution until April, but you do have to take another distribution in the same year. You could end up taking two distributions in the same year to meet that requirement, therefore, most people don't elect to defer their first year distribution, but that's an option.

How it works: If you turned 70 1/2 in 2019, you could defer that distribution until April 1, 2020, but then you have to meet the second requirement of distribution in 2020 as well by the end of the year. Now with the recently passed SECURE Act you are able to wait until age 72 before required minimum distributions must begin if you were not yet age 70 ½ by January 1, 2020.

Age 59½—Diversifying the 401(k)

At age 59½, most employers allow for what is called an *in-service distribution*, which allows you to begin diversifying your 401(k) assets that you have with your employer. In fact, you can roll over the entire 401(k) balance to an IRA and take more control over it, investing it in whatever way you choose or begin funding your income strategies for retirement early.

This rule really comes from the Enron days, when employees were forced to hold company stock and were unable to diversify it. Then, when stocks went down, a lot of lawsuits occurred. The solution provided the ability, when you're 59½, to begin diversifying those assets, take more control, get less risky assets, and purchase retirement income solutions. It's a great age to solidify your retirement plan if you have not done so already.

Principle 8

Maximizing Leftovers

> *You can retire from a job, but don't ever retire from making extremely meaningful contributions in life.*
>
> —*Stephen Covey*

The earlier you're able to identify that assets will be left over, the more you can maximize them. If you realize you're able to generate enough income to support the lifestyle you want in retirement, and you have sufficient assets in your growth quadrant that will enable you to keep pace with inflation, then you may be able to maximize your estate. You may determine, "There's just no way in the world I'm going to spend all of these assets during retirement, and there's going to be a lot left over." If so, you have identified an opportunity to create an estate plan, to maximize the amount your heirs will receive.

That is a really powerful concept, so I'm going to repeat it: *The earlier you're able to identify that assets will be left over, the more you can maximize them.* The ultra-rich use this strategy to help maximize what they leave to their heirs. They take millions of dollars that they know will pass to the next generation and buy life insurance, which delivers three or four times the amount tax-free. That's right, since life insurance is tax-free, there will be no income tax due on the death benefits. Also, the high-net-worth individuals purchase the life insurance inside an entity called an *irrevocable life insurance trust*, to prevent estate taxes as well.

The wealthy take those assets, multiply them, and leave them completely tax-free to their heirs, creating much more wealth for the next generation. If the intention is to leave a lot of assets behind, the sooner you identify that you have extra resources, the better you can strategize ways to leave lots more assets for your heirs.

Estate Planning

Regardless of your objective and whether or not you plan to spend your last dime, you will need several estate-planning documents to make it easier to handle last wishes and leftover property.

What are the estate-planning documents that are typical in any estate plan? The recommended documents for an effective estate plan are the Last Will and Testament, Durable Power of Attorney, Medical Power of Attorney, HIPAA Authorization and Release, Directive to Physicians (also known as a Living Will), Declaration of Guardian in the Event of Later Incapacity or Need of Guardian, and Appointment of Agent for Disposition of Remains. If you require more control over the assets or want to gain more privacy over your estate, you may benefit by setting up a Revocable Living Trust as well.

Last Will and Testament

The most familiar document in your estate plan is the *Last Will and Testament*. A Will designates what happens to your property when you die and who are the rightful new owners of your property. A Will is not effective until after you die and a judge signs an Order declaring the Will to be valid and appointing the Executor to serve. This court process administering estates is called *probate*.

Probate is a necessary process to ensure an efficient and proper distribution of your estate after you die. The process allows the Court to safeguard and protect Wills and determine heirs in estates where there is no Will (which is referred to as *intestate*). The probate process confirms that there are no outstanding debts, liens or judgments and that no one else has a claim to your property, other than the beneficiaries named in the Will or the legal heirs to your estate.

Having a Will in place and making sure your Will meets all legal requirements of the state you live in is extremely important. Each state has different rules about how your documents should be worded to help the probate process go as smoothly (and inexpensively) as possible.

The benefits to having a Will are endless; however, if you die without a Will, there is a legal process to determine the distribution of your estate to your legal heirs.

Many people assume that if they die without a Will, their assets will go to the state. Fortunately, this is an incorrect assumption. If you do not have a Will, then the intestacy laws determine who your legal heirs are and who inherits your property. The intestacy laws typically meet most people's intentions. However, if you have children from outside your current marriage when you die, some of your property may end up being co-owned between your spouse and your children. This is often not an ideal situation. Therefore, Wills are extremely important for blended families.

Durable Powers of Attorney

The Statutory Durable Power of Attorney appoints an agent to act on your behalf with regard to your finances and is the most important document in your estate plan. Unfortunately this document is often overlooked, even though it is arguably more important than a Will. The Durable Power of Attorney says who can step into your shoes and act in your name with regard to all of your financial affairs, including, among other things, managing your bank accounts, paying your bills, and even buying and selling real property. The *durable* component allows the document to stay in effect even if you become incapacitated. If you're in a coma, someone can still act in your name to handle your financial affairs. Without the Durable Power of Attorney, no one is authorized to sign your name or handle your financial affairs unless you have otherwise authorized them.

Most people automatically assume that they can handle all of their loved ones' financial affairs because of the way their bank accounts are set up. For example, if you have a joint account with rights of survivorship, you have authorized the co-owner (typically your spouse) to access that account for any purpose during your lifetime. The rights of survivorship means that it belongs solely to the co-owner after your death. This is a contractual agreement with the bank that trumps your Will and your Durable Power of Attorney. Upon your death, the co-owner provides the bank the death certificate, completes their forms, and then the co-owner becomes the sole owner of the account, regardless of what your Will provides. Because most spousal accounts are contractual set up as joint tenancy with a right of survivorship, people often assume that they can handle things for their loved ones because of that one contractual agreement that they have with the bank. However, they neglect to see that this agreement only applies to that one account and not the entire estate.

The biggest problems arise with investment accounts and retirement accounts. Retirement accounts, such as 401(k)s and IRAs, can only be in your name individually (after all, it is called an *individual* retirement account, and therefore it can't be joint). If something happens to you and you become incapacitated, your spouse or loved ones cannot access any funds in the IRA without a separate specific authorization with that financial institution or a Durable Power of Attorney. Even if your loved one is the beneficiary of that account, that only gives them the right to receive the account after you die, but it does not allow the beneficiary access to the account while you are living. A Durable Power of Attorney, in this case, would be imperative to allow your loved ones to access the account in order to pay your bills, take your required minimum distributions, and manage your account accordingly.

Selling real property is another circumstance where a Durable Power of Attorney is imperative. To close a sale, all owners of real property must sign and agree to it. Many married couples assume that since they are married and both own the property, one of them automatically has the legal rights to singlehandedly give consent to the sale. That is incorrect. Remember, no one has the legal authority to act on your behalf, sign your name, or do anything financially for you unless you have authorized them by contract with the financial institution or named them as your agent on your Durable Power of Attorney. If you become incapacitated, your loved ones, including your spouse, will not be able to act on your behalf financially without this authority.

The Durable Power of Attorney may convey authority to your agent to act on your behalf effective immediately or effective only when you are deemed incapacitated. Additionally you can make limitations relating to the scope of authority conveyed in the document. Will you only allow your agent to pay your bills and file your taxes? Or are you going to allow your agent to have additional power to fully act on your behalf without limitation? You should only name agents whom you trust to step into your shoes and act in accordance with your wishes. If you are not willing to allow your agent the full authority to act immediately, then you should rethink whom you are appointing as your agent. Afterall, if you do not trust your agent to act while you have capacity, then why would you trust them to act when you are incapacitated? Additionally, making the Durable Power of Attorney effective only upon your disability or incapacity will at minimum cause a delay in granting your agent the authority to act and potentially render the document ineffective, if a doctor is unwilling to certify in writing that you are unable to manage your financial affairs.

Naming agents on your Durable Power of Attorney is an extremely important decision and should only be done after consulting with an attorney and evaluating all the specific circumstances of your wishes, your estate, and your family dynamics. While it is common for people to appoint their eldest child first, this is not always the wisest choice. You must carefully consider a lot of things before you choose the best person to handle practical financial matters. For every agent and successor agent you name, you should ask: What does the agent do for a living? How long have they been employed? Where do they live? Are they good with finances? Do they manage their own finances in a way that you manage your own? Have they filed for bankruptcy? After answering these questions, the eldest child or the one who wants to be in charge is often not the best choice.

It may seem like an easy task to appoint someone to handle your finances, but it is not quite effortless. You have to make sure the person you're appointing is not only trustworthy and responsible but also has your best interest at heart.

Medical Powers of Attorney

The second most important document is your Medical Power of Attorney. Unlike the Durable Power of Attorney, which appoints a financial agent to make decisions for you, the Medical Power of Attorney appoints an agent to make health care decisions for you. This document is only effective upon your disability or incapacitation. As long as you are able to make decisions regarding your health, luckily, you get to make them. It is only if you are unconscious, incapacitated, in a procedure, or do not understand some medication or a physician's explanation that your named medical power of attorney can make those decisions for you.

Keep in mind that this document falls number two on the list, not number one, because there is actually a default provision under the law. The Texas statute provides that doctors can turn to your spouse first to make medical decisions for you. If you don't have a spouse, they can turn to your adult children or your parents to make it for you. Problems can arise with this if your adult children do not get along, disagree on the medical treatment, or do not have your best interest at heart.

More often than not, people try to hold off the idea of death and dying until they actually have to think about it. The *Medical Power of Attorney* allows you to appoint someone to make medical decisions for you when you are no longer capable of doing so and is important to ensure that the right person is making medical decisions for you so that your wishes are followed.

HIPAA Authorization and Release

HIPAA (Health Insurance Portability and Accountability Act of 1996) is a federal law that requires security standards for the protection of medical and other types of healthcare information. Individuals who have access to your healthcare information are prohibited from releasing such information without your express approval. You can name individuals you trust to have access to this protected information in a HIPAA Release and Authorization.

When you execute a HIPAA Release and Authorization, you give your healthcare providers permission to discuss your health information with the individuals you have named. This can be an important tool for those who are assisting you with your healthcare and want to stay informed of your status. This document also allows you to keep others who are close to you informed of your medical condition, even if they cannot make decisions.

Directive to Physicians / Living Will

Along with the Medical Power of attorney, a *Directive to Physicians and Family or Surrogates*, more commonly known as *Living Will, is an important part of your estate plan*. Many people confuse this document with the actual Will or Last Will and Testament; however, this document is effective when you are alive and outlines your wishes about being provided life-sustaining treatment. A Directive to Physicians provides information and instructions regarding your desires to administer, withhold, or withdraw life-sustaining treatment should you be diagnosed with a terminal or irreversible condition. A Living Will is typically executed before the onset of illness or incapacity. It serves as a guideline regarding your preferred medical care and whether or not you want to be provided life support if you are incapacitated and either have a terminal condition or an irreversible condition, whether or not you want to undergo dialysis or to be unplugged or stay plugged in indefinitely. Outlining your wishes in the Directive to Physicians is very important so that your Medical Power of Attorney can direct your care in a difficult, potentially end-of-life, decision.

Although commonly confused, a Living Will is not the same as a Do Not Resuscitate Order ("DNR"). A DNR should be signed only after receiving an explanation from a physician, who also signs the document to confirm you were provided the information necessary to make a sound decision. While a Living Will addresses life-sustaining treatment before your heart has stopped beating, a DNR instructs medical personnel not to perform emergency resuscitation after your heart has stopped beating. Importantly, if you have a properly executed DNR, medical personnel must see it prior to beginning resuscitation procedures, as they cannot stop resuscitation procedures once they have begun.

Declaration of Guardian in the Event of Later Incapacity and Need of Guardian

A *guardianship* is a process whereby the Court will appoint somebody to act on your behalf in instances of incapacity. The Court legally removes a person's rights to act. The Declaration of Guardian in the Event of Later Incapacity and Need of Guardian is a document that is used in the court proceeding for a guardianship that designates who you want to serve as guardian of the person (i.e. similar to the Medical Power of Attorney) or guardian of the estate (i.e., similar to a Durable Power of Attorney). If you have a Durable Power of Attorney and a Medical Power of Attorney, most people will never need a guardian. However, there are instances where the powers of attorney do not work or do not convey enough authority for your agent to act. In those instances, a guardianship may be necessary if you become incapacitated and need protection. Most instances requiring a guardianship involve exploitation and abuse. Therefore, it is good to have this document to fully set forth your wishes in case you are taken advantage of.

Do I Need a Revocable Living Trust?

A Revocable Living Trust is essentially a contract that governs the management and distribution of your assets during your lifetime and after death with regard to the assets that are funded in the trust. If you have a Revocable Living Trust AND it is fully funded with all of your assets, you can potentially avoid having to go through probate proceedings. Additionally, a Trust appoints a trustee who manages the assets of the Trust. When the trustee dies, the successor trustee steps up seamlessly to manage the Trust assets in lieu of an agent acting as your Durable Power of Attorney. Some banks and financial institutions prefer the role of trustee over an agent under a Power of Attorney allowing your loved ones to handle your affairs without having to jump through hoops. A Revocable Living Trust can also be beneficial for large estates or for families who do not get along.

Having a *Revocable Living Trust can be helpful in some circumstances, but is not always necessary.* For example, if you have property in multiple states, having a Revocable Living Trust would be advisable in order to potentially avoid having to go through probate proceedings in multiple states. But if you are probating in only one state that does not have state estate taxes, like Texas, many find that the cost of creating a trust and the undertaking to make sure it is properly funded and managed is not worthwhile. From a cost standpoint, you might not save much if anything at all by trying to avoid probate with a trust. Additionally, many people that have a Revocable Living Trust to avoid probate fail to fund the trust completely and end up having to probate anyway.

Another reason people prefer a Revocable Living Trust is for privacy. When you probate a Will, it is a public proceeding. Because a trust transfers assets by contract, it remains private.

A Revocable Living Trust is a complicated contract that can be expensive. Most people do not benefit from having a Revocable Living Trust. However, it can be beneficial in certain specific situations. Before creating a Revocable Living Trust, you should make sure you understand your objectives and fully understand the tradeoffs and benefits of having a trust.

What to Expect from an Estate-Planning Attorney

When meeting with an estate-planning attorney, you should show up with a list of your financial accounts, assets and objectives. Think about what you want to happen to your assets, who you want to handle your financial affairs, and who you want to handle your medical decisions. It is important to be prepared to discuss the pool of people you trust to make decisions for you and a clear list of objectives of what you want to happen to your assets. You should also be prepared with a list of your bank accounts and assets, including how the assets are titled and if they have beneficiary designations. The estate-planning attorney should discuss all of your family dynamics in order to guide you on the right documents for your circumstances and the best way to accomplish your objectives.

Deferring to the advice of your estate-planning attorney is important. There is a lot of bad information online. Although most estate planning documents are available through LegalZoom or other online platforms, self-planning without legal advice can backfire, particularly in times of crisis. It is smart to have a general understanding of estate planning; however, googling *trusts* and *Wills* will not necessarily provide you with the best legal advice. The laws vary from state to state so relying on the advice of a public figure may not always provide the appropriate plan. Ultimately, the more control you retain over your assets after you die and the more complex estate plan you create could cause more problems, lead to a higher legal fee, and over complicate a simple estate. Discussing all the possibilities with an estate-planning attorney and developing a plan together is the smartest and best way to proceed to ensure a successful and thorough estate plan.

Other Ways to Transfer Assets

Some assets can transfer directly to your beneficiaries without having to go through the probate process. Life insurance, annuities, 401(k)s, pensions, and IRAs may pass by contractual agreement with the financial institution using a beneficiary designation. There is a sequence of how assets are transferred, and a listed beneficiary is always first priority. In fact, if you have listed an ex-spouse as a beneficiary, the asset could transfer to the ex-spouse depending on whether that asset is controlled by federal or state law. The beneficiary designation trumps your Will or Trust and is imperative to evaluate when developing your estate plan.

The next way assets are transferred is by title. If you have a bank account and it's labeled *transfer on death* (TOD) or *payable on death* (POD), that account will be paid to the person listed as the TOD or POD at your death. Title will transfer to the person listed after providing a death certificate to the financial institution. Like the beneficiary designation accounts, these accounts pass by contractual agreement with the financial institution. They do not pass through your Will or Trust and are not subject to the probate proceedings.

If you have listed a beneficiary or *payable on death* designation on accounts and you change your Will, you must make sure that the beneficiary and POD designations still coincide with your wishes or are intentionally different than those set forth in your Will. If any of your accounts do not pass by POD title or by beneficiary, then they will pass through your Will or estate in the probate proceedings.

The Importance of Elder Law Planning

Although everyone over the age of 18 needs estate planning, particularly a Durable Power of Attorney, Medical Power of Attorney, and HIPAA Authorization, many people do not realize the importance of these documents until later in life. As we age and need more assistance from others, it can be very helpful to engage the specialized expertise of an elder law attorney. And, if you are in the position of helping loved ones as they age, then you need to ensure that you are obtaining advice from attorneys with experience in the area of serving seniors.

These days, it is very difficult for an attorney to be a "jack of all trades." The laws have become too complex. When it comes to the needs of seniors, many people, including many attorneys, do not know what they do not know. Over the past 20 years, "elder law" has developed as a separate area of the law due to the unique and complex issues faced by older persons and persons with disabilities. Elder law attorneys help seniors and their families plan for and react to issues involved with aging and the need for long-term care, including understanding Medicare, Medicaid, VA benefits and other public benefits programs, health and long-term care insurance, health care decision-making, the drafting of special needs and other trusts, selection of long-term care providers, home care and nursing home problem solving, retiree health and income benefits, and fiduciary services and representation in addition to drafting of estate planning documents. Elder law attorneys who comply with the National Academy of Elder Law Attorneys (NAELA) aspirational standards understand and empathize with the physical and mental difficulties that accompany the aging process. Elder law attorneys also have a broad understanding of the various laws that impact a situation with the goal of preventing future problems and maximizing the quality of life for seniors.

Seniors make up the fastest growing segment of the population, with more than 10,000 people turning 65 every day. Unfortunately, that means that seniors are increasingly vulnerable to those who are looking for an easy profit. It also means that more and more individuals will have had some sort of experience with some of these issues and will have an "expert opinion" based on that limited experience. Often nothing can be more damaging than an opinion that is based on limited experience with a limited understanding of the ramifications of an action.

Elder Abuse and exploitation are rampant. Our senior population is being targeted by lottery schemes and bad actors. It is imperative that we watch out for and are involved in our loved ones' lives so that we can protect them from abuse. If your loved one is getting older and can't handle his or her own finances, it is important to begin to watch the accounts and obtain a power of (Collins 2011)attorney. Ensure you have beneficiaries on all accounts possible, including bank accounts, and that you have a foolproof method to allow heirs and your executor to access all your digital assets. (Where are the passwords stored? Can they get to them?) Do not assume their phone or computer will be available! Consult with the proper professionals to protect your loved ones and prevent exploitation and abuse before it happens.

Principle 9

Live a Life without Limits

> I want to be thoroughly used up when I die. Life is no brief candle to me; it is a sort of splendid torch which I get ahold of for the moment and I want to make it burn as brightly as possible before handing it on to future generations.
>
> —George Bernard Shaw

You may not be sure what to think about the chapter titled "Live a Life Without Limits," especially coming after previous chapters about spending less and saving more. However, the most powerful human ability is the freedom of choice—the freedom to choose and make decisions that will determine your future, decisions that will open opportunities, and decisions that will restrict them. The consequences for all decisions you make today are multiplied over time and will either create greater or lesser opportunities. There is no reality of just maintaining the status quo. Financially, if you choose not to save early, then it will limit what you can do with your future income, as you will be required to play catch-up by saving more later or learn to reduce your lifestyle once you can no longer work. There is no escaping the outcomes of our choices.

I think you'll find that all life's decisions are that way; the outcomes are magnified over a lifetime. Developing the right financial habits early will enable you to be prepared for the unexpected and allow you to not only have more choices but better options that come from having the financial resources necessary to overcome many of life's challenges.

A Great Example: Megan Getrum

Megan Getrum exemplified the benefits of living a life without limits. Megan was disciplined and worked hard early on, as she graduated from high school in 1999 as class valedictorian. For college, she chose an in-state school and her performance was good enough to win an academic scholarship to cover a lot of her expenses. Megan graduated from UT Dallas in the spring of 2003 with a Bachelor of Science in computer science and started her independent life debt free. Her first job was with Raytheon in Garland, Texas; her second was with Masergy in Plano, Texas.

Megan always lived within her means, and she paid off her credit card bill every month. She enrolled in the 401(k) plans at work and saved money in her other "no touchy" savings account. She also consistently built a separate reserve fund for larger unexpected expenses like car repairs or quick trips. She drove the same car for many years, and when she was ready, she bought herself a new car and paid cash. When she met her untimely death at age thirty-six, she had an estate valued over $785,000.

Saving all the money did not stop her from enjoying life, traveling, and making new friends. Her budget included annual passes to her yoga studio and several concerts every year. She enjoyed saving and using her money. Her international travels included tours in Scotland, Ireland, Machu Picchu in Peru, India, as well as many trips within the United States. Her parents felt she had a knack for balancing pleasure and thrift.

It could be easy to think that maybe Megan should have spent more during her lifetime, as saving could have been less of a priority. However, the security of having the resources she had was the very essence, which enabled her to live her best financial life. She experienced the freedom that comes from practicing the principles in this book. As the great Abraham Lincoln said: "And in the end, it's not the years in your life that count. It's the life in your years."

What It Means to Live a Life without Limits

To live a life without limits is to have the freedom to seek out more life experiences and do the things you want or are passionate about. It's doing things "just because," rather than having to do something because of a paycheck and financial obligations. It's having the resources to live out those dreams and not being limited by financial barriers. It's pursuing your passions during retirement, whether it's starting your own business or volunteering your time.

Retirement is a time for pursuing your passions. One reason it's a good time is that retirement provides a less risky way to pursue your passions, since you are already secure financially.

One of my retired clients, Ernest Marcos, is finally able to spend more time developing his artistic abilities in writing and music. Each day he wakes up and goes for a walk, while letting his creative side develop short stories, new characters, and ideas for his new novel. When he returns home, he types out all the ideas he had on his walk, which has enabled him to finish two full books of fictional short stories as well his first novel. In an interview, he explained, "The writing game is a lot of fun for me. I loved reading, and now I enjoy writing too." What a great example of living your best financial life.

He is leveraging the freedom he enjoys each day to create something new from whatever he can imagine. He also explains, "I love recording songs. I meet really good jazz musicians who are just fun, really fun guys. And we sit around, and we play, and we record. I have always been a decent artist, and now, in retirement, I've kind of gotten back to it. I go to a couple of classes, since there's a lot of adult sort of educational classes. You get to draw ideas of things that you have of whatever suits you. And I go to meet people because you become friends. My wife recently had a birthday, and we had it on the beach nearby, and there were almost forty people who came to the party, and most of the people we've met since we moved to Miami after retirement. Some are lawyers, pediatricians, some of them play instruments, and sometimes we get together for music or whatever. I am thoroughly enjoying retirement life. Every day does feel like a Saturday, but I actually don't know when it's Saturday or Monday. I go to supermarkets and stand in the checkout counter and ask, 'What day is it, by the way?' I also get to spend a lot of time with family. I have young grandchildren, and that's a lot of fun, to be with them."

How Will You Spend Your Time during Retirement?

It's probably one of the most important questions I ask near-retirees: How will you spend your time during retirement? Specifically, I ask them, "What will you do in retirement that you can't do while you are working? Why is it necessary you quit your job and turn off the paycheck?" Many times, they don't have an answer or haven't taken the time to plan their time like they have planned their finances.

When you have worked a thirty- or forty-year career, imagining a world without that job may be difficult. But it's very important before you retire to ask yourself: What will you do on Monday? What will you do with your time? What have you been getting from the job in terms of a sense of importance or accomplishment and maybe some social perks? What are the benefits of your job besides the paycheck? Make a list of the benefits of your job besides the paycheck.

Then, determine where you'll receive those same rewards once you have retired. Many clients find that volunteering and helping others through charitable work fulfills the role of feeling important and helps them feel that they make a difference. Community and charitable work are a great avenue, and so are fishing, traveling, golfing, craft-making, working in the garage, and other activities that keep you productively busy.

If you think the honey-do list is going to keep you busy forever, it won't. A few months or years into retirement, you may have caught up on the projects and find yourself looking for more meaningful and fun things to do in your postcareer life. Start developing your hobbies and interests before you retire, so you'll have an easier transition.

Finding New Challenges

I have worked a lot with engineers who are the top 1 percent of engineers globally, and they like to solve problems and have a sense of accomplishment. For many, it's crucial to identify those next projects, the next problems they're going to be able to help solve so that they stay engaged, happy, and keep their minds active in retirement.

Finding those things before they retire will enable them to have a great retirement and not end up going back to work simply because they don't have a sense of purpose.

Ken Robinson makes a stark distinction between leisure and recreation. He states in his insightful book *The Element:*

> There's an important difference between leisure and recreation. In a general sense, both words suggest processes of physical or mental regeneration.

> But they have different connotations. Leisure is generally thought of as the opposite of work. It suggests something effortless and passive. We tend to think of work as something that takes our energy. Leisure is what we do to build it up again. Leisure offers a respite, a passive break from the challenges of the day, a chance to rest and recharge. Recreation carries a more active tone—literally of re-creating ourselves. It suggests activities that require physical or mental effort, but which enhance our energies rather than the depleting them. (2009, 218)

The key is finding an activity that you're passionate about and energizes you to actively participate in meaningful recreation in retirement. Most people don't retire to do something, but rather to escape something at work. The necessity for something greater than leisure will usually manifest itself in time.

> On-the-job stress is cited as the number-one reason for employee dissatisfaction in the American workforce.
>
> 40 percent of Americans say their job is "very or extremely stressful" ... and 42 percent say the stress interferes with their family or personal lives.
>
> The prime causes of all this stress ... are low pay, commuting, unreasonable workload, and fear of being fired or laid off. (Adler 2013)

Financial Health Includes Your Health

Retirement can be great for your physical health, depending on how you use your time. Work stress, on the other hand, can be the opposite. "Studies have found that unhappiness at work has a significant negative impact on one's health ... psychosocial factors—like work-related stress—represent the single most important variable in determining how long somebody lives." (Adler 2013)

If retirement is so great, why is it so easy to procrastinate planning for it? There is actually a very good reason, and it has to do with the way our brains are developed. In the book *Pitch Anything*, which I consider a masterpiece and a must-read, author Warren Klaff explains that your brain first filters ideas through a primitive process. He states, "It [your brain] is trying to determine whether the information coming in is a threat [to your] immediate survival and, if it isn't, whether it can be ignored without consequence" (2011). Retirement planning isn't urgent and can be easily ignored for a long time without consequence, until it becomes a part of your immediate survival and it is too late. The benefits and personal rewards for developing the discipline to review your plan for retirement and confirm you are on track are powerful, motivating, and freeing.

As they say, early in your career you trade your health for wealth and then spend the later years trying to trade your wealth for health. One client succinctly stated, "The thing that I was relaxed about, I think a lot of people are, is physical fitness. You have a financial fitness, and you have to have consciousness about that, but don't cheat yourself physically. You don't have to become a bodybuilder, but do something, even if it is nothing more than just walk every day. I decided to retire, as I spent many hours each day driving to each sales meeting, and eventually I couldn't get in and out of the car anymore. I wish I would have managed my health as diligently as I managed my money."

I think making good financial decisions and developing healthy eating and exercise habits go hand in hand. Both require personal discipline to make sacrifices in the short term for long-term results. Besides, what good is building your net worth for a great future if you're not healthy enough to enjoy it?

What Will You Be Remembered Most For?

What will you be remembered most for when you're gone? What will you have wished you'd spent more time doing? As they say, "Nobody on their death bed wishes they would have spent more time at the office" (H. Jackson Brown 1991). Instead, they wish they would have spent more time with their families and loved ones. Retirement is a great opportunity to develop those relationships with family, grandkids, and the community.

Conclusion

It's interesting to examine why some people thrive in retirement, as well as financially throughout their lives, while others struggle from paycheck to paycheck. There are five primary areas of discipline that can determine whether you are on track to your best financial life.

1. Cash-flow management: the ability to spend less than you make and maintain an adequate emergency fund
2. Investment choices: the ability to focus on low-cost investment options and maintain the proper asset allocation
3. Lifestyle constraint: the ability to withstand impulsive behavior and maintain frugality
4. Risk management and contingency planning: the ability to obtain proper insurance protection for your assets and plan for unexpected events
5. Sense of purpose or importance: the ability to stay active and relevant, which will improve your quality of life and longevity

Successful retirement planning can be paralleled to the lessons learned from early twentieth-century explorers. In 1911, two groups of explorers journeyed to the South Pole in an adventure many called "the race to the end of the earth." There was no means of communication—no cellular phones, no radios, and no channel to call a base camp or a rescue team. One group, led by Roald Amundsen, used one key to thrive in their endeavor to success:

discipline. Every day, the group would walk twenty miles toward their goal to reach the pole. When weather conditions were favorable, some team members suggested they walk a few miles more. But Amundsen, who understood the value of rest, would stick to only twenty miles per day. The next day, a storm let loose its fury and unleashed gale-force winds. It was freezing cold and tough to catch sight of the path. Still, the group braved the weather and walked twenty miles, regardless. It went on like that for the rest of their journey, twenty miles every day.

Their counterpart group, led by Robert Scott, had a different approach. When weather was pleasant, he would lead his team to walk as far as they could, pushing their team to the brink of exhaustion, and would end up covering about forty to sixty miles and sometimes even more. During harrowing conditions, they would either walk a mile or two or just spend the entire day in their tents, writing in their journals and waiting for the weather to improve.

Who would reach the pole first? Would either of them make it home? After a few months on the excursion, Scott's group finally made it to the South Pole—thirty-four days late. Amundsen's group had already mounted flags and was heading back home—again, with their consistent twenty-mile march. Scott's group, on the other hand, maintained their practice: trek farther on days when weather is excellent and wallow in tents when conditions get ugly. In the end, Amundsen's group made it home. Unfortunately for Scott's group, the advancing winter swallowed them up, and all of them perished. (Collins 2011)

You don't have to be aggressive to get to retirement, but be disciplined and consistent in your approach. As you implement each of these principles in your own financial planning, remember that mastery is an ongoing process and requires frequent review, recalculation, and adaption as the environment changes. But developing the discipline to follow the process and work on it will enable you to experience your best financial life. So get started and create more Saturdays!

Works Cited

Adler, Maynard Webb and Carlye. 2013. *Rebooting Work*. San Franscisco, CA: Jossey-Bass A Wiley Imprint.

Bollin, Phillip E. (2017). Title: Warren Buffett declares himself the winner of the "million-dollar bet". Retrieved June 9, 2017 from http://bollinwealth.com/2017/03/warren-buffett-declares-himself-the-winner-of-the-million-dollar-bet/

Botsford, Erin. 2012. *The Big Retirement Risk*. Austin, TX: Greenleaf Book Group Press.

Collins, Jim and Hansen, Morten T. 2011. *Great By Choice*. HarperCollins.

Covel, Michael W. 2011. *The Little Book of Trading*. Hoboken, NJ: John Wiley & Sons, Inc.

H. Jackson Brown, Jr. 1991. *Life's Little Treasure Book On Success*. Nashville, TN: Rutledge Hill Press, Inc.

Hansen, Jim Collins and Morten T. 2011. *Great By Choice*. New York, NY: Harper Business.

Hinden, Stan. 2013. *How to Retire Happy*. New York, NY: McGraw Hill.

Ibbotson, Roger G. and Kaplan, Paul D. 2000. "Does Asset Allocation Policy Explain 40, 90 or 100 Percent of Performance?" *Financial Analysts Journal*.

IFSE (2017). Title: Understand the difference between active vs. passive investing. Retrieved June 9, 2017 from (IFSE, 2017)

Ken Robinson, Ph.D. 2009. *The Element*. Strand: Penguin Books Ltd.

Klaff, Oren. 2011. *Pitch Anything*. McGraw Hill.

LeVitre, Ray E. 2010. *20 Retirement Decisions You Need to Make Right Now*. Naperville, IL: Sphinx Publishing.

Malkiel, Burton G. 2007. *A Random Walk Down Wall Street*. New York, NY: W.W. Norton & Company.

Milevsky, Moshe A. 2012. *The 7 Most Important Equations for Your Retirement*. Ontario Canada: John Wiley and Sons Canada, Ltd.

Morning Edition. Title: Armed with an index fund, Warren Buffett is on track to win hedge fund bet. Retrieved June 9, 2017 from http://www.npr.org/2016/03/10/469897691/armed-with-an-index-fund-warren-buffett-is-on-track-to-win-hedge-fund-bet

Pfau, Wade D. 2013. *The Lifetime Sequence of Returns: A Retirement Planning Conundrum*. Abstract, McLean: SSRN.

Pfau, Wade. 2017. *How Much Can I Spend In Retirement?* McLean, VA: Retirement Researcher Media.

Roiter, Bill. 2008. *Beyond Work*. Mississauga: John Wiley & Sons Canada, Ltd.

Solin, Daniel R. 2009. *The Smartest Retirement Book You'll Ever Read*. New York, NY: Penguin Group.

Steinberg, Judith B. Harrington and Stanley J. 2007. *The Everything Retirement Planning Book*. Avon, MA: Adams Media. (Milevsky 2012)

Swedroe, Lee (2011). Title: The difference between active management and passive management. Retrieved June 9, 2017 from http://www.cbsnews.com/news/the-difference-between-active-management-and-passive-management/
And
http://fortune.com/2017/12/30/warren-buffett-million-dollar-bet/